uthors: Marie-France Cecchini, Magaly Baudel, Maria Hoffmann-Dartev
raphic Design: Kathrin Mosandl
ditorial: Emily Bernath, Juergen Lorenz, Bert Weaver

30	
31	
32	trente-deux tranNt-dun
40	quarante kah-rahNt
50	cinquante saNk-ahNt
60	soixante swah-sahNt
70	soixante-dix swah-sahNt-deess
80	quatre-vingts kah-truh-vaN
90	quatre-vingt dix kah-truh-vaN deess
100	cent sahN
101	cent un sahNt-aN
102	cent deux sahN-duh
110	cent dix sahN-deess
111	cent onze sahNt-ohNz
120	cent vingt sahN-vaN
200	deux cent duh sahN
300	trois cent trwah sahN
400	quatre cent kah-truh sahN
437	quatre cent trente-sept kah-truh-sahN-trahNt-set
1000	mille meel
2000	deux mille duh meel
10.000	dix mille dee meel
100.000	cent mille sahN meel
1.000.000	un million aN meel-yohN

ISBN 978-3-468-98942-1
Printed in Germany

The Basics

Good afternoon!	Bonjour! bohN-zhoor
Good evening!	Bonsoir! bohN-swahr
Goodbye!	Au revoir. oh-ruh-vwah
…, please!	…, s'il vous plaît. see voo play
Thank you.	Merci. mehr-see
Yes.	Oui. wee
No.	Non. nohN
Sorry!	Excusez-moi. ex-kew-zeh-mwah
Get a doctor / an ambulance, quick!	Appelez vite un médecin / une ambulance! ah-play veet aN mad-saN / ewn ahN-bew-lahNs
Where are the restrooms?	Où sont les toilettes? oo sohN lay twah-let
When?	Quand? kahN
What?	Quoi? kwah
Where?	Où? oo
Here.	Ici. ee-see
There.	Là-bas lah bah
On the right.	À droite. ah drwaht
On the left.	À gauche. ah gohsh
Do you have …?	Avez-vous…? ah-veh-voo
I'd like …	J'aimerais bien… zhem-eh-reh bee-aN
How much is that?	Ça coûte combien? sah koot kohN-bee-aN
Where is …?	Où est…? oo eh
Where can I get …?	Où est-ce-qu'il y a…? oo es-keel yah

III

Langenscheidt

Pocket Phrasebook French

with Travel Dictionary and Grammar

Langenscheidt

Berlin · Munich · Vienna · Zurich
London · Madrid · New York · Warsaw

Table of Contents

Table of Contents

Shopping _____ 103

Table of Contents

When different gender forms apply, the masculine form will be indicated by ♂, the feminine form by ♀. Therefore, a man would say: Je suis ♂ heureux. A woman would say: Je suis ♀ heureuse.

Bye!	Salut! sah-lew
It was nice meeting you.	Je suis ♂ heureux / ♀ heureuse d'avoir fait votre / ta connaissance. zhuh swee uhr-uh / uhr-uhz dah-vwah feh vo-truh / tah cohN-nay-sahns
Thank you for a lovely *evening / day*.	Merci pour cette charmante *soirée / journée*. mehr-see poor set shahr-mahNt swah-ray / zhoor-nay

The pronunciation of each word is given. Simply read it as if it were an English word. See also simplified pronunciation guide pages 10-12.

Sometimes you see two alternatives in italics, separated by a slash. Choose the one that is appropriate for the situation, e.g. soirée for evening or journée for day.

yourself?	comment va? koh
What's your name?	Comment *vous appelez-vous / tu t'appelles*? koh-mahN voo-zah-play voo / tew-tah-pel

French has a formal (form.) and informal (inform.) way to address people. See also grammar section page 204.

8

The arrow indicates where you find additional expressions.

If there is more than one way to continue a sentence, any of the possibilities that follow can be inserted.

➤ *Accepting / Declining an Invitation, page 22*

Where's the nearest …	Où est … *le / la* plew p … *luh / lah* plew p
— subway station?	— la station de métro lah stah-see-ohN duh may-troh
— bus stop?	— l'arrêt d'autobus lah-ray-do-toh-bewss
Which *bus / subway* goes to …?	*Quel bus / quel métro* va à …? kel bewss / kel may-tro vah ah
Where is the bus stop to …?	Où est l'arrêt d'autobus pour…? oo eh lah-ray do-toh-bewss poor
e bus numéro …	The bus number …
a ligne …	The … line.
re there discounts for…?	Est-ce qu'il y a une réduction pour …? es-keel ya ewn ray-dewk-see-ohN poor
o I have to transfer to get o …?	Pour …, est-ce que je dois changer? poor… es-kuh zhuh dwah shahN-zheh
ould you tell me where I	Pouv … dois desc … veh voo

You can insert your choice of word(s) from the Additional Words section in place of ellipses marks.

Phrases that you may hear but may never say are shown in reverse, with French on the left side.

Pronunciation

This section is designed to make you familiar with the sounds of
French. You'll find the pronunciation of the French letters and
sounds explained below, together with their "imitated"
equivalents. Simply read the pronunciation as if it were English,
noting any special rules below.

Consonants

Letter	Approximate Pronunciation	Symbol	Example	Pronunciation
ch	like sh in shut	sh	chercher	shehrshay
ç	like s in sit	s	ça	sah
g	1) before e, i, y, like s in pleasure	zh	manger	mangzhay
	2) before a, o, u, like g in go	g	garçon	gahrsawN
gn	like ni in onion	n	ligne	leen
h	always silent		homme	om
j	like s in pleasure	zh	jamais	zhahmay
qu	like k in kill	k	qui	kee
r	rolled in the back of the mouth, like gargling	r	rouge	roozh
w	usually like v in voice	v	wagon	vahgawN

Vowels

a, à or â	between the a in hat and the a in father	a/ah	mari	mahree
é or ez	like a in late	ay	été	aytay
è, ê, e	like e in get	e/eh	même	mem
e	sometimes like er in other	er	je	zher
i	like ee in meet	ee	il	eel
o	generally like o in hot	o/oh	donner	donnay
ô	like o	o/oh	Rhône	rohn
u	like ew in dew	ew	cru	krew

───── Pronunciation ─────

Letters b, c, d, f, k, l, m, n, p, s, t, v, x and z are pronounced as in English.

Sounds spelled with two or more letters

Letter	Approximate Pronunciation	Symbol	Example	Pronunciation
ai, ay,	can be pronounced	ay	j'ai	zhay
aient, ais,	like *a* in l*a*te or		vais	vay
ait, aî, ei	like *e* in g*e*t	e/eh	chaîne	shen
			peine	pen
(e)au	similar to o	o/oh	chaud	sho
eu, eû, œu	like *ur* in f*ur*, but with lips rounded, not spread	ur	peu	pur
euil, euille	like *uh* in h*uh*, but without pronouncing the *h* and with a *y* sound added	uhy	feuille	fuhy
ail, aille	like *ie* in t*ie*	ie	taille	tie
oi, oy	like w followed by the a in hat	wa	moi	mwah
ou, oû	like o in move or oo in hoot	oo	nouveau	noovo
ui	approximately like wee in between	wee	traduire	trahdweer

Nasal Sounds

French contains nasal vowels, which are transcribed with a vowel symbol plus N. This N should not be pronounced strongly but is included to show the nasal quality of the previous vowel. A nasal vowel is pronounced simultaneously through the mouth and the nose.

11

Liaison

Normally, final consonants of words are not pronounced in French. However, when a word ending in a consonant is followed by one beginning with a vowel, they are often run together, and the consonant is pronounced as if it began the following word.

Examples:

nous	*noo*
nous avons un enfant	*noo zavawN zaN nahngfahN*
comment	*komahN*
Comment allez-vous?	*komahN-tah-lay-voo*

Stress

All syllables in French are pronounced with more or less the same degree of stress (loudness). Stress has not been indicated in the phonetic transcription and each syllable should be pronounced with equal stress.

Pronunciation of the French Alphabet

A	ah		N	en
B	bay		O	o
C	say		P	pay
D	day		Q	kew
E	er		R	ehr
F	ef		S	ess
G	zhay		T	tay
H	ahsh		U	ew
I	ee		V	vay
J	zhee		W	dooblervay
K	kah		X	eex
L	el		Y	ee grek
M	em		Z	zed

Meeting People

How are you?
Comment allez-vous?

Fine, thanks.
Très bien, merci.

Communication Difficulties

Do you speak English?
Parlez-vous anglais?
pah-lay voo ahN-glay

Does anyone here
speak English?
Est-ce que quelqu'un ici parle
anglais? es-kuh kel-kaN ee-see pahrl
ahN-glay

Did you understand
that?
Vous avez compris?
vooz-ah-veh kohN-pree

I understand.
J'ai compris. zheh kohN-pree

I didn't understand
that.
Je n'ai pas compris.
zhuh nay pah kohN-pree

Could you speak a bit
more slowly, please?
Vous pourriez parler un peu plus
lentement, s'il vous plaît? voo poor-
ee-eh pah-lay aN puh plew lahN-tuh-
mahN see voo-play

Could you repeat that?
Vous pourriez répéter?
voo poor-ee-eh ray-pay-teh

What does ... mean?
Que veut dire ...? kuh vuh deer

Could you write it
down for me?
Vous pourriez me l'écrire?
voo poor-ee-eh muh lay-creer

Greetings

Good morning / afternoon! Bonjour! bohN-zhoor

Good evening!
Bonsoir! bohN-swah

Goodnight!
Bonne nuit! bun nwee

Hello!
Salut! sah-lew

— Meeting People —

info Greetings vary according to how well you know someone. It's polite to shake hands, both when you meet and say good-bye. Good friends sometimes give each other a hug, and women kiss each other on the cheeks.

How are you?	**Comment allez-vous / vas-tu?** koh-mahN-tah-lay-voo / vah-tew
How are things?	**Comment ça va?** koh-mahN sah-vah
Fine, thanks. And you?	**Très bien, merci. Et vous?** tray bee-aN mehr-see eh voo
I'm afraid I have to go now.	**Je suis désolé, mais je dois partir maintenant.** zhuh swee day-zo-lay may zhuh dwah pah-teer maN-tuh-nahN
Goodbye!	**Au revoir!** oh-ruh-vwah
See you *soon / tomorrow*!	**A *bientôt / demain*!** ah *bee-aN-toh / duh-maN*
Bye!	**Salut!** sah-lew
It was nice meeting you.	**Je suis ♂ heureux / ♀ heureuse d'avoir fait votre connaissance.** zhuh swee ♂ uhr-uh / ♀ uhr-uhz dah-vwah feh vo-truh kohN-nay-sahN
Thank you for a lovely *evening / day*.	**Merci pour cette charmante *soirée / journée*.** mehr-see poor set shahr-mahNt *swah-ray / zhoor-nay*
Have a good trip!	**Bon voyage!** bohN vwah-yazh

info There are two forms for "you" (taking different verb forms): tu (informal / singular) is used when talking to relatives, children, close friends and between young people. Vous (formal, singular and plural) is used in all other cases.

Getting to Know Each Other

Introductions

What's your name?	Comment *vous appelez-vous* / *tu t'appelles*? koh-mahN *voo-zah-play voo* / *tew-tah-pel*
My name is …	Je m'appelle … zhuh mah-pel
May I introduce …	Permettez-moi de vous présenter. C'est … pehr-met-teh-mwah duh voo pray-sahN-teh say
– my husband.	– mon mari. mohN mah-ree
– my wife.	– ma femme. mah fahm
– my (boy)friend.	– mon ami. mohN-nah-mee
– my (girl)friend.	– mon amie. mohN-nah-mee

info The terms ami ♂ and amie ♀ define a friend, not necessarily a boyfriend or girlfriend.

Where are you from?	D'où *venez-vous* / *viens-tu*? doo *vuh-nay-voo* / *vee-aN tew*
I'm from …	Je viens … zhuh vee-aN
– the US.	– des États-Unis. day-zeh-tah-sew-nee
– Canada.	– du Canada. dew kah-nah-dah
– the UK.	– du Royaume-Uni. dew rwah-yohm-ew-nee

How old are you?	**Quel âge *avez-vous* / *as-tu*?** kel ahzh *ah-veh-voo* / *ah tew*
I'm …	**J'ai … ans.** zheh … ahN
Are you married?	***Êtes-vous* / *Es-tu* marié?** *et-voo* / *eh-tew* mah-ree-eh
Do you have any children?	**Avez-vous des enfants?** ah-veh-voo day-zaN-fahN

Asking Someone Out

➤ *Accepting / Declining an Invitation, page 18*

Would you like to go out *tonight* / *tomorrow*?	**Si on se voyait *ce soir* / *demain*?** see ohN suh vwa-yeh *suh swah* / *duh-maN*
We could do something together, if you like.	**On pourrait faire quelque chose ensemble, si vous le voulez.** ohN poor-eh fehr kel-kuh shoze ahN-sahN-bluh see voo voo-lay
Would you like to have dinner together tonight?	**Si on dînait ensemble ce soir?** see ohN dee-nay ahN-sahN-bluh suh swah

➤ *Nightlife, page 167*

I'd like to take you out.	**Je voudrais vous inviter.** zhuh voo-dray voo-zaN-vee-teh
Would you like to go dancing?	**Voulez-vous aller danser?** voo-lay-voo ah-lay dahN-say
What time should we meet?	**On se donne rendez-vous à quelle heure?** ohN suh done rahN-day-voo ah kel uhr

Let's meet at …	Disons qu'on se rencontre à … heures. dee-zohn kohN suh rahN-kohN-truh ah … uhr
I'll take you home.	Je vous raccompagne jusque chez vous. zhuh voo rah-kohN-pahn-yuh zhews-kuh sheh voo
Could we meet again?	On va se revoir? ohN vah suh ruh-vwah

Accepting / Declining an Invitation

I'd love to.	Très volontiers. treh vol-ohN-teeyeh
OK.	O.K., d'accord. oh-keh dah-kaw
I don't know yet.	Je ne sais pas encore. zhuh nuh say pah-zahN-kaw
Maybe.	Peut-être. puh-tet-truh
I'm sorry, but I can't.	Je suis désolé, mais je ne peux pas. zhuh swee day-zo-lay may zhuh nuh puh pah
I'm already doing something.	J'ai déjà quelque chose de prévu. zheh day-zhah kel-kuh shoze duh pray-vew

Flirting and Romance

► *Asking Someone Out, page 17*

| Did you come by yourself? | Vous êtes ♂seul / ♀seule ici? voo-zet suhl ee-see |
| Do you have a *boyfriend / girlfriend*? | As-tu *un ami / une amie*? ah-tew aN-nah-mee / ew-nah-mee |

18

You're very beautiful.	Tu es magnifique. tew eh mahnee-fee-kuh
I like you.	Je t'aime bien. zhuh tem-bee-aN
I love you.	Je t'aime. zhuh tem
Are you coming back to my place?	Tu viens chez moi? tew vee-aN sheh mwah
Leave me alone!	Laissez-moi tranquille! lay-say mwah traN-kee

Polite Expressions

Expressing Likes and Dislikes

Very good!	Très bien! treh bee-aN
I'm very happy.	Je suis très ♂ content / ♀ contente. zhuh swee treh ♂ kohN-taN / ♀ kohN-taNt
I like that.	Ça me plaît. sah-muh-play
What a shame!	Dommage! doh-mazh

I'd rather …	**J'aimerais mieux …** zhem-eh-reh myuh
I don't like it.	**Ça ne me plaît pas.** sahn nuh muh play pah
I'd rather not.	**Je ne préfèrerais pas.** zhuh nuh pray-fehr-eh pah
Certainly not.	**En aucun cas.** ahN oh-kaN kah

Expressing Requests and Thanks

Thank you very much.	**Merci beaucoup.** mehr-see bo-koo
May I?	**Vous permettez?** voo pehr-met-teh
Please, …	**S'il vous plaît, …** see-voo-play
No, thank you.	**Non, merci.** nohN mehr-see
Could you help me, please?	**Est-ce que vous pourriez m'aider, s'il vous plaît?** es-kuh voo poor-ee-eh meh-day see-voo-play
Thank you. That's very nice of you.	**Merci beaucoup. C'est très aimable de votre part.** mehr-see bo-koo seh treh-zem-ah-bluh duh vo-truh pah
You're welcome.	**Il n'y a pas de quoi.** eel nee-ah pahd-kwah

Apologies

Sorry!	**Pardon!** pahr-dohN
Excuse me!	**Excusez-moi!** ex-kew-say mwah
I'm sorry about that.	**Je suis désolé.** zhuh swee day-zo-lay

20

Don't worry about it!	Ça ne fait rien! sahn nuh feh ree-aN
How embarrassing!	C'est très embarrassant pour moi! seh treh-zahN-bah-rahs-sahN poor mwah
It was a misunderstanding.	C'était un malentendu. say-teh aN mah-lahN-tahn-dew

Meeting People: Additional Words

address	l'adresse *f* lah-dress
alone	seul suhl
to be called; my name is	s'appeler; je m'appelle sah-play; zhuh mah-pel
to be from	venir de vuh-neer duh
boy	le garçon luh gah-sohN
boyfriend	l'ami *m* lah-mee
brother	le frère luh frehr
brothers and sisters	les frères et sœurs *m/pl* lay-frehr eh suhr
child	l'enfant *m* lahN-fahN
to come back	revenir ruh-vuh-neer
country	le pays luh pay-ee
daughter	la fille la fee
engaged	fiancé fee-ahN-say
father	le père luh pehr
free	libre lee-bruh
friend	l'amie *f* lah-mee
friend	l'ami *m* lah-mee
girl	la jeune fille lah zhuhn fee
girlfriend	l'amie *f* lah-mee
to go dancing	aller danser ah-lay dahN-say
to go out to eat	aller manger ah-lay mahN-zheh
husband	le mari luh mah-ree

21

to invite	inviter aN-vee-teh
to like	aimer em-eh
to make a date	se donner rendez-vous
	suh dun-nay rahN-day-voo
married	marié mah-ree-eh
to meet	faire la connaissance de
	fehr lah koh-nay-sahNs duh
to meet	se rencontrer suh rahN-kohN-tray
mother	la mère lah mehr
Mr.	Monsieur muh-syuh
Ms.	Madame ma-dahm
partner	le compagnon / la compagne luh
	kohN-pahn-yohN / la kohN-pahn-yuh
photo	la photo lah fo-toh
please	s'il vous plaît see voo-play
to repeat	répéter ray-pay-teh
school	l'école *f* lay-cuhl
sister	la sœur lah suhr
slowly	lentement lahN-tuh-mahN
son	le fils luh feess
to speak	parler pah-lay
student	l'étudiant / l'étudiante
	lay-tew-dyahN / lay-tew-dyahNt
to study	faire des études fehr day-zeh-tewd
thank you	merci mehr-see
to understand	comprendre kohN-prahN-druh
vacation	les vacances *f/pl* lay vah-kahNs
to wait	attendre ah-tahN-druh
wife	la femme la fahm

Accommodations

Where's the tourist information office?
Où se trouve l'office du tourisme?

The key to room ..., please.
La clé de la chambre ..., s'il vous plaît.

Lodging

Looking for a Room

Where's the tourist information office?

Où se trouve l'office du tourisme?
oo suh troov law-feess dew toor-eez-muh

Can you recommend …

Vous pourriez me recommander …
voo poor-ee-eh muh ruh-kohN-mahN-day

– a good hotel?
– a reasonably priced hotel?
– a bed & breakfast?

– un bon hôtel? aN bohn o-tel
– un hôtel pas trop cher?
 aN-no-tel pah tro shehr
– une pension? ewn pahN-see-ohN

Could you make a reservation for me?

Vous pourriez réserver pour moi?
voo poor-ee-eh ray-sehr-veh poor mwah

Is it far from here?

C'est loin d'ici? say lwahN dee-see

HOTEL DU POULDU

24

How do I get there?	Comment est-ce que je peux m'y rendre? koh-mahN es kuh zhuh puh mee rahN-druh

Arriving

I have a reservation. My name is …	On a retenu chez vous une chambre à mon nom. Je m'appelle … ohN ah ruh-ten-ew sheh voo ewn shahN-bruh ah mohN nohN zhuh mahpell
Do you have a *double / single* room …	Vous auriez une chambre pour *deux personnes / une personne* … voo-zoh-ree-eh ewn shahN-bruh poor *duh pehr-sun / ewn pehr-sun*
– for one night?	– pour une nuit? poor ewn nwee
– for … nights?	– pour … nuits? poor … nwee
– with a bathroom?	– avec salle de bains? ah-vek sahl-duh-baN
– with a balcony?	– avec balcon? ah-vek bahl-kohN
– with air conditioning?	– avec climatisation? ah-vek klee-mah-tee-zah-see-ohN
– with a fan?	– avec un ventilateur? ah-vek vahN-tee-lah-tuhr
– with an ocean view?	– avec vue sur la mer? ah-vek vew sewr lah mehr

info All types of accommodations can be found through the **Office du Tourisme / Syndicat d'initiative**, the tourist information center.

Malheureusement, nous sommes complets.	I'm afraid we're booked.

How much is it …	Combien ça coûte … kohN-bee-aN sah koot
– with breakfast?	– avec le petit déjeuner? ah-vek luh puh-tee day-zhuhn-eh
– without breakfast?	– sans le petit déjeuner? sahN luh puh-tee day-zhuhn-eh
– with breakfast and lunch or dinner?	– avec la demi-pension? ah-vek lah duh-mee pahN-see-ohN
– with all meals included?	– avec la pension complète? ah-vek lah pahN-see-ohN kohN-plet
Do you offer a discount if I stay … nights?	Est-ce qu'il y a une réduction, si l'on reste … nuits? es-keel-yah ewn ray-dewk-see-ohN see lohN rest … nwee

▶ *Numbers, see inside front cover*

Can I see the room?	Je pourrais voir la chambre? zhuh poor-eh vwah lah shahN-bruh
Could you put in an extra bed?	Vous pourriez installer un lit supplémentaire? voo poor-ee-eh aN-stah-lay aN lee sew-pluh-mahN-tehr
Do you have another room?	Vous auriez encore une autre chambre? voo-zo-ree-eh ahN-kaw ewn o-truh shahN-bruh
It's very nice. I'll take it.	Elle me plaît. Je la prends. el muh play zhuh lah prahN
Could you take my luggage up to the room?	Vous pourriez apporter mes bagages dans la chambre? voo-poor-ee-eh ahp-paw-teh may bah-gahzh dahN lah shahN-bruh

Where's the bathroom?	Où sont les toilettes? oo sohN lay twah-let
Where can I park my car?	Où est-ce que je peux garer ma voiture? oo es kuh zhuh puh gah-ray mah vwah-tewr
Between what hours is breakfast served?	Jusqu'á quelle heure est servi le petit déjeuner? zhews-kah kel huhr eh sehr-vee luh puh-tee day-zhuh-nay
Where's the dining room?	Où est la salle à manger? oo eh lah sahl ah mahN-zheh

Service

Can I leave my valuables with you for safekeeping?	Est-ce que je peux vous confier mes objets de valeur? es kuh zhuh puh voo kohN-fee-eh may-zob-zheh duh vah-luhr
I'd like to pick up my valuables.	Je voudrais reprendre mes objets de valeur. zhuh voo-dreh ruh-praN-druh may-zob-zheh duh vah-luhr
The key to room …, please.	La clé de la chambre …, s'il vous plaît. lah clay duh lah shahN-bruh … see voo play
Can I call the US/UK from my room?	Est-ce que je peux téléphoner aux États-Unis / en Grande-Bretagne de ma chambre? es kuh zuh puh tel-eh-foh-nay o-zeh-tah-zew-nee / ahN grand-bruh-tahn duh mah shahN-bruh
Are there any messages for me?	Est-ce qu'il y a un message pour moi? es keel-yah aN mes-sahzh poor mwah

Could I have …, please?	**Est-ce que je peux avoir…, s'il vous plaît?** es kuh zhuh puh ah-vwah … see-voo-play
– an extra blanket	**– une couverture supplementaire** ewn koo-vehr-tewr sew-pluh-mahN-tehr
– an extra towel	**– une serviette supplementaire** ewn sehr-vee-et sew-pluh-mahN-tehr
– a few more hangers	**– quelques porte-vêtements supplementaires** kel-kuh pawt-vet-mahN sew-pluh-mahN-tehr
– an extra pillow	**– un autre oreiller** aN o-truh aw-ray-eh
The window won't *open / close*.	**La fenêtre ne *s'ouvre / ferme* pas.** lah fuh-net-ruh nuh *soo-vruh / fehrm* pah
… doesn't work.	**… ne marche pas.** nuh mahsh pah
– The shower	**– La douche** lah doosh
– The TV	**– La télévision** lah teh-lay-vee-see-ohN

28

– The heat	– Le chauffage luh sho-fahzh
– The Internet connection	– La connexion à Internet lah koh-nek-see-ohN ah aN-tehr-net
– The air conditioning	– La climatisation lah klee-mah-tee-zah-see-ohN
– The light	– La lumière lah lewm-yehr
The *drain / toilet* is clogged.	*Le lavabo est bouché. / Les toilettes sont bouchées.* luh lah-vah-bo eh boo-sheh / lay twah-let sohN boo-sheh
… is dirty.	… est sale. eh sahl

Departure

Please wake me at … (tomorrow morning).	Réveillez-moi (demain matin) à … heures, s'il vous plaît. ray-feh-yeh-mwah (duh-maN mah-taN) ah … uhr see-voo-play
We're leaving tomorrow.	Nous partons demain. noo pah-tohN duh-maN
May I have my bill, please?	Préparez-nous la note, s'il vous plaît. prey-pah-ray-noo lah note see-voo-play
It was very nice here.	Nous avons passé un séjour très agréable. noo-zah-vohN pahss-eh aN say-zhoor treh-zah-gray-ah-bluh
Can I leave my luggage here until …?	Est-ce que je peux encore laisser mes bagages ici jusqu'à … heures? es kuh zhuh puh ahN-kaw less-eh may bah-gahzh ee-see zhuhsk-ah…uhr
Please call me a taxi.	Appelez-moi un taxi, s'il vous plaît. ah-play-mwah aN tahx-ee see voo play

Rentals

We've rented apartment …

Nous avons loué l'appartement …
noo-zah-vohN loo-eh lah-paht-uh-mahN

Je pourrais avoir votre bon de réservation?

Could I have your coupon / voucher, please?

Where do we get the keys?

Où pouvons-nous prendre les clés?
oo poo-vohN-noo prahN-druh lay clay

info The 220-volt / 50-cycle AC is universal in France, Belgium, and Switzerland. Buy an adapter with round, not square, pins if you bring electrical appliances. If they cannot be switched to 220 volts you'll also need a transformer appropriate to the wattage of the appliance.

Could we please have some (extra) *bed linens* / *dish towels*?

Nous pourrions avoir *des draps* / *des torchons* (en plus)? noo poor-ee-ohN ah-vwah *day drah* / *day taw-shohN* (ahN plews)

Could you show us how … works, please?

Vous pourriez nous expliquer comment fonctionne …, s'il vous plaît? voo poor-ee-eh noo-zex-plee-keh kohN-mahN fohNk-see-un … see-voo-play

– the dishwasher
– the stove
– the washing machine
– the dryer

– le lave-vaisselle luh lahv-veh-sel
– la cuisinière lah kwee-zeen-yehr
– la machine à laver
  lah mah-sheen ah lah-veh
– le séchoir luh say-shwahr

Where does the garbage go?

Où devons-nous déposer les ordures? oo duh-vohN-noo day-po-zeh lay-zaw-dewr

Where's …

Où se trouve … oo suh troov

– the nearest bus stop?
– a supermarket?

– a bakery?

– le prochain arrêt de l'autobus?
  luh pro-shaN ah-reh duh lo-to-bewss
– un supermarché?
  aN sew-pehr-mahr-sheh
– une boulangerie?
  ewn boo-lahN-zheh-ree

Camping

Is there room for …?

Est-ce qu'il y a encore de la place pour…? es keel yah ahN-kaw duh lah plahss poor

31

How much is it for ...

Quel est le tarif pour ...
kel eh luh tah-reef poor

– ... adults and ... children?

– ... adultes et ... enfants?
... ah-dewlt eh ... ahN-fahN

– a car with a trailer?

– une voiture avec caravane?
ewn vwah-tewr ah-vek kah-rah-vahn

– an RV (recreational vehicle)?

– un camping-car?
aN kahN-ping kah

– a tent?

– une tente? ewn tahNt

Do you also rent out *bungalows* / *trailers*?

Est-ce que vous louez aussi des *bungalows* / *caravanes*? es kuh voo loo-eh o-see day *bahN-gah-lo* / *cah-rah-vahn*

We'd like to stay for *one day* / ... *days*.

Nous voudrions rester *un jour* / ... *jours*. noo voo-dree-ohN res-teh *aN zhoor* / ... *zhoor*

Where can we *put up our tent* / *park our trailer*?

Où pouvons-nous installer *notre tente* / *notre caravane*? oo poo-vohN-noo aN-stah-lay *no-truh tahNt* / *no-truh kah-rah-vahn*

Where are the *bathrooms* / *restrooms*?

Où sont les *lavabos* / *toilettes*? oo sohN lay *lah-vah-bo* / *twah-let*

Where can I empty the chemical toilet?

Où est-ce que je peux vider les toilettes chimiques? oo es-kuh zhuh puh vee-day lay twah-let shee-meek

Is there an electric hookup?

Vous avez un branchement électrique? voo-zah-veh aN brahNsh-mahN eh-lek-treek

32

Can I *buy / exchange* propane tanks here?

Je peux *acheter / échanger* des bouteilles de butane ici? zhuh puh *ahsh-teh / eh-shahN-zheh* day boo-teh duh bew-tahn ee-see

Rentals, page 30

Accommodations: Additional Words

adapter	l'adaptateur *m* lah-dahp-tah-tuhr
advance booking	la réservation lah ray-sehr-vah-see-ohN
apartment	le studio luh stew-dyoh
armchair	le fauteuil luh fo-tuh-yuh
ashtray	le cendrier luh sahN-dree-eh
bathtub	la baignoire lah behn-wah
bed	le lit luh lee
bed linen	les draps *m/pl* lay drah
bedspread	la couverture lah koo-vehr-tewr
bill	la facture lah fahk-tewr
breakfast room	la salle du petit déjeuner lah sahl dew puh-tee day-zhuh-nay
broken	cassé kah-say
broom	le balai luh bah-lay
bulb	l'ampoule *f* lahN-pool
bunk beds	les lits *m/pl* superposés lay lee sew-pehr-po-say
to camp	camper kahN-per
camping	le camping luh kahN-ping
campsite	le terrain de camping luh tehr-aN duh kahN-ping
chair	la chaise lah shehz
check-in	la déclaration de séjour lah day-clah-rah-see-ohN duh say-zhoor

33

cleaning products	les produits *m/pl* de nettoyage
	lay pro-dwee duh neh-twhah-yazh
coffee-maker	la cafetière (électrique)
	lah kah-feh-tyehr (eh-lek-treek)
complaint	la réclamation
	lah ray-klah-mah-see-ohN
cot (for a child)	le lit d'enfant luh lee dahN-fahN
deposit	l'acompte *m* lah-kohNt
deposit	la caution lah ko-see-ohN
detergent	la lessive lah less-eev
dirty	sale sahl
dishes	la vaisselle lah veh-sel
dormitory	le dortoir luh daw-twah
double bed	le lit conjugal
	luh lee kohN-zhew-gahl
drain	l'écoulement lay-kool-mahN
drinking water	l'eau *f* potable lo po-tah-bluh
dryer	le sèche-linge luh sehsh-laNzh
elevator	l'ascenseur *m* lah-sahN-suhr
emergency exit	la sortie de secours
	lah sor-tee duh suh-koor
extension cord	la rallonge électrique
	lah rah-lohNzh eh-lek-treek
extra week	la semaine supplémentaire
	lah suh-men sew-pluh-mahN-tehr
faucet	le robinet luh raw-bee-neh
fireplace	la cheminée lah shuh-mee-nay
firewood	le bois de chauffage
	luh bwah duh sho-fahzh
floor	l'étage *m* lay-tazh
foam mattress	le tapis de sol luh tah-pee duh sol
fuse	le fusible luh few-zee-bluh
garbage can	la poubelle lah poo-bel
gas canister	la cartouche de gaz
	lah kah-toosh duh gahz

34

gas stove	le réchaud à gaz luh ray-sho ah gahz
glass	le verre luh vehr
hammer	le marteau luh mahr-to
hanger	le cintre luh saN-truh
to iron	repasser ruh-pah-say
lamp	la lampe lah lahNp
laundry room	les lavabos *m/pl* lay lah-vah-bo
to leave	partir pah-teer
lobby	le hall d'entrée luh ahl dahN-tray
lounge	la salle de réunion
	lah sahl duh ray-ewn-yohN
to make reservations	réserver ray-sehr-veh
mattress	le matelas luh maht-lah
minibar	le minibar luh mee-nee-bah
mirror	la glace lah glahss
mosquito coil	la spirale anti-moustiques
	lah spee-rahl ahN-tee-moo-steek
mosquito net	la moustiquaire lah moos-tee-kehr
off-peak season	la basse saison lah bahss say-sohN
outlet	la prise (de courant)
	lah preez (duh koo-rahN)
peak season	la haute saison lah oht say-sohN
phone	le téléphone luh tel-eh-fohn
plug	la fiche lah feesh
range	la cuisinière lah kwee-seen-yehr
reception	la réception lah ray-sep-see-ohN
refrigerator	le réfrigérateur
	luh ray-free-zheh-ah-tuhr
rent	le loyer luh lwah-yeh
to rent	louer loo-eh
rental fee	le prix de la location
	luh pree duh lah lo-kah-see-ohN
reserved	réservé ray-sehr-veh
room	la chambre lah shahN-bruh
RV (recreational vehicle)	le camping-car luh kahN-ping kah

safe	le coffre-fort luh kawf-ruh for
sheet	le drap luh drah
single bed	le lit à une place
	luh lee ah ewn plahss
sink	le lavabo luh lah-vah-bo
sleeping bag	le sac de couchage
	luh sahk duh-koo-shahzh
stove	le réchaud luh ray-sho
swimming pool	la piscine lah pee-seen
table	la table lah tah-bluh
tent	la tente lah tahNt
tent peg	le piquet (de tente)
	luh pee-keh (duh tahNt)
terrace	la terrasse lah teh-rahss
toilet paper	le papier hygiénique
	luh pah-pyeh ew-zhen-eek
toilet / restroom	les toilettes *f/pl* lay twah-let
trailer	la caravane lah kah-rah-vahn
TV room	la salle de télévision
	lah sahl duh teh-lay-vee-see-ohN
vacation home	la maison de vacances
	lah may-sohN duh vah-kahNs
voltage	le voltage luh vol-tahzh
wardrobe	l'armoire *f* lahr-mwah
washing machine	la machine à laver
	lah mah-sheen ah lah-veh
water	l'eau *f* lo
window	la fenêtre lah fuh-net-ruh
youth hostel	l'auberge *f* de jeunesse
	lo-behrzh duh zhuh-ness
youth hostel ID	la carte d'adhérent des auberges
	de jeunesse la kahrt dah-dehr-rahN
	day-zo-behrzh duh zhuh-ness

Travel

Excuse me, where's …?
Pardon, où est …?

Is this seat taken?
Est-ce que cette place est occupée?

Asking for Directions

Excuse me, where's …?	**Pardon, où est …?** pah-dohN oo eh
How do I get to …?	**Pour aller à …?** poor ah-lay ah
Could you please show me on the map?	**Vous pouvez me le montrer sur la carte, s'il vous plaît?** voo poo-veh muh luh mohN-treh sewr lah kahrt see voo play
How many minutes *on foot / by car*?	**C'est à combien de minutes *à pied / en voiture*?** say ah kohN-bee-aN duh mee-newt *ah pyeh / ahN vwah-tewr*
Is this the road to …?	**C'est bien la route pour …?** say bee-aN lah root poor
How do I get onto the expressway to …?	**Comment arriver sur l'autoroute pour …?** kohN-mahN ah-ree-veh sewr lo-toh-root poor
Je suis désolé, je ne sais pas.	I'm afraid I don't know.
La *première / deuxième* rue à *gauche / droite*.	The *first / second* road on your *left / right*.
Au prochain *feu / croisement* …	At the next *traffic light / intersection* …
Traversez *la place / la rue* …	Cross the *square / street* …
Vous pouvez prendre *le bus / le métro*.	You can take the *bus / subway*.

Where Is It?

à côté de	beside / next to
à droite	right / to the right
à gauche	left / to the left
assez loin	quite a long way
croisement *m*, carrefour *m*	intersection
derrière	after / behind
devant	before / in front of
en arrière	back
en bas de l'escalier	down the steps
en face de	opposite
en haut de l'escalier	up the steps
feu *m*	traffic lights
ici	here
là-bas	there
la rue	street
la route	road
par ici	this way
par là	over there
pas loin	not far
près de	nearby
tout droit	straight ahead
virage *m*	bend

Luggage / Baggage

I'd like to leave my luggage here.	Je voudrais laisser mes bagages ici. zhuh voo-dray less-eh may bah-gahzh ee-see
My luggage hasn't arrived (yet).	Mes bagages ne sont pas (encore) arrivés. may bah-gahzh nuh sohN pah (zahN-kaw) ah-ree-veh
Where's my luggage?	Où sont mes bagages? oo sohN may bah-gahzh
My suitcase has been damaged.	Ma valise a été abîmée. mah vah-leez ah eh-teh ah-bee-may
Whom should I speak to?	A qui est-ce que je peux m'adresser? ah kee-es-kuh zhuh puh mah-dress-eh

At the Airport

Where's the … desk?	Où est le guichet de la compagnie aérienne …? oo eh luh gee-sheh duh lah kohN-pahn-yee ah-ehr-ee-en
How much is a flight to …?	Combien coûte un vol pour …? kohN-bee-aN koot aN vol poor
A … ticket, please.	Un billet …, s'il vous plaît. aN bee-yeh… see voo play
– one-way	– aller simple ah-lay saN-pluh
– round-trip	– aller-retour ah-lay-ruh-tour
– business class	– en classe affaire ahN klahss ah-fehr

▶ *Numbers, see inside front cover*

I'd like *a window* / *an aisle seat*.	J'aimerais bien une place *côté fenêtre* / *côté couloir*. zhem-eh-reh bee-aN ewn plahss *ko-teh fuh-neh-truh* / *ko-teh kool-wahr*
Can I take this as a carry-on?	Est-ce que je peux prendre cela comme bagages à main? es-kuh zhuh puh prahN-druh suh-lah kom bah-gahzh ah maN
I'd like to ... my flight.	Je voudrais ... mon vol. zhuh voo-dreh ... mohN vol
– confirm	– reconfirmer ruh-kohn-feer-may
– cancel	– annuler ah-newl-lay
– change	– modifier mo-dee-fyeh

Airport: Additional Words

airport	l'aéroport *m* lah-ehr-o-por
airport shuttle bus	la navette (d'aéroport) lah nah-vet (dah-ehr-o-por)
airport tax	la taxe d'aéroport lah tahx dah-ehr-o-por
arrival	l'arrivée *f* lah-ree-veh
boarding pass	la carte d'embarquement lah cahrt dahN-bahrk-mahN
check-in desk	le guichet luh gee-sheh
connecting flight	la correspondance lah kah-rehs-ohN-dahNs
delay	le retard luh ruh-tahr
departure	le départ luh day-pahr
exit	la sortie lah saw-tee
flight attendant	le steward / l'hôtesse de l'air *f* luh stew-ahr / lo-tess duh-lehr
flying time	la durée du vol lah dew-ray dew vol

41

landing	l'atterrissage _m_ lah-tehr-ee-sahzh
local time	l'heure _f_ locale luhr lo-kahl
pilot	le pilote luh pee-lot
plane	l'avion _m_ lah-vee-ohN
return flight	le vol de retour luh vol duh ruh-tewr
sick bag	le sachet en cas de nausée
	luh sah-sheh ahN kah duh no-zeh
stopover	l'escale _f_ les-kahl

Travel by Train

Information and Tickets

Where can I find the _baggage storage / lockers_?

Où est la _consigne / consigne automatique_? oo eh lah _kohN-seen-yuh / kohN-seen-yuh o-toh-mah-teek_

When's the next train to …?

A quelle heure part le prochain train pour …? ah kel uhr pahr luh pro-shaN traN poor

When does it arrive in …?

A quelle heure arrive-t-il à …? ah kel uhr ah-reev-teel ah

Do I have to change trains?

Je dois changer? zhuh dwah shahN-zheh

Which track does the train to … leave from?

De quel quai part le train pour …? duh kel keh pahr luh traN poor

Are there discounts for …

Est-ce qu'il y a une réduction pour … es-keel ya ewn ray-dewk-see-ohN poor

– families?
– children?
– students?

– les familles? lay fah-mee
– les enfants? lay-zahN-fahN
– les étudiants? lay-zeh-tew-dyahN

A ... ticket to ..., please.

Un billet ... pour ..., s'il vous plaît.
aN bee-yeh ... poor ... see voo play

– one way
– round trip
– child fare
– adult

– aller simple ah-lay saN-pluh
– aller retour ah-lay ruh-tour
– pour enfants poor ahN-fahN
– pour adultes poor ah-dewlt

I'd like to reserve a seat.

Je voudrais réserver une place.
zhuh voo-dreh ray-zehr-veh ewn plahss

I'd like ...

Je voudrais ... zhuh voo-dreh

– a window seat.

– une place à côté de la fenêtre.
ewn plahss ah ko-teh duh lah fuh-neh-truh

– an aisle seat.

– une place à côté du couloir.
ewn plahss ah ko-teh dew kool-wah

– non-smoking
– smoking

– non-fumeur nohN-few-muhr
– fumeur few-muhr

I'd like to take my bicycle with me.

Je voudrais emporter mon vélo.
zhuh voo-dreh ahN-paw-teh mohN veh-lo

info Validate your ticket at the train station by inserting it in an orange machine - machine à composter or composteur. Otherwise you may get fined by the conductor.

At the Train Station

Accès aux quais	To the platforms
Consigne automatique	Lockers
Douches	Showers
Eau non potable	Non-potable water
Eau potable	Drinking water
La consigne	Baggage Storage

43

La sortie	Exit
Renseignements	Information
Restaurant de la gare	Station Restaurant
Salle d'attente	Waiting room
Toilettes	Restrooms
Voie	Track

On the Train

Is this the train to …?	C'est le train pour …? say luh traN poor
Is this seat taken?	Est-ce que cette place est occupée? es-kuh set plahss eh-tawk-ew-pay
Excuse me, that's my seat.	Excusez-moi, c'est ma place. ex-kew-zeh-mwah say mah plahss
Could you help me, please?	Est-ce que vous pouvez m'aider, s'il vous plaît? es-kuh voo poo-veh meh-day see voo play
Do you mind if I open / close the window?	Vous permettez que j'ouvre / je ferme la fenêtre? voo pehr-meh-teh kuh zhoo-vruh / zhuh fehrm lah fuh-neh-truh
How many more stops to …?	Combien y a-t-il encore d'arrêts jusqu'à …? kohN-bee-aN yah-teel ahN-kaw dah-reh zhews-kah
How long does the train stop here?	Combien de temps dure l'arrêt? kohN-bee-aN duh tahN dewr lah-reh
Will I catch my connection to …?	Est-ce que j'aurai le train pour …? es-kuh zhoh-ray luh traN poor

44

Travel by Train: Additional Words

arrival	l'arrivée *f* lah-ree-veh
car	la voiture lah vwah-tewr
class	la classe lah klahss
compartment	le compartiment luh kohN-pahr-tee-mahN
conductor	le contrôleur luh kohN-tro-luhr
connection	la correspondance lah koh-res-pohN-dahNs
departure	le départ luh day-pahr
dining car	le wagon-restaurant luh vah-gohN-res-toh-rahN
exit	la sortie lah saw-tee
fare	le prix du billet luh pree dew bee-yeh
luggage car	le wagon à bagages luh vah-gohN ah bah-gahzh

non-smoking
  compartment
	le compartiment non-fumeurs luh
	    kohN-pahr-tee-mahN nohN few-muhr

platform	le quai luh keh
reserved	réservé ray-zehr-veh
schedule	l'horaire *m* lo-rehr
seat	la place lah plahss
sleeper car	le wagon-lit luh vah-gohN-lee
smoking compartment	le compartiment fumeurs luh kohN-pahr-tee-mahN few-muhr
surcharge	le supplément luh sewp-pluh-mahN
to arrive	arriver ah-ree-veh
to change trains	changer de train shahN-zheh duh traN
to get off	descendre day-sahN-druh
to get on	monter mohN-teh
track	voie vwah
train	le train luh traN
train station	la gare lah gahr

Travel by Bus

How do I get to the bus station?	Comment est-ce que je peux faire pour aller à la gare routière? kohN-mahN es-kuh zhuh puh fehr poor ah-lay ah lah gahr roo-tyehr
When does the next bus to … leave?	Quand part le prochain car pour…? kahN pahr luh pro-shaN kahr poor
A ticket / Two tickets to …, please.	Un ticket / Deux tickets pour …, s'il vous plaît. aN tee-keh / duh tee-keh poor… see voo play
Could you tell me where I have to get off?	Pouvez-vous me dire où je dois descendre? poo-veh-voo muh deer oo zhuh dwah day-sahN-druh
How long does the trip last?	Combien de temps dure le voyage? kohN-bee-aN duh tahN dewr luh vwah-yahzh

info Tickets can normally be purchased from the bus driver, but you must always validate your ticket in the machine (composter votre billet).

Travel by Boat

Information and Reservations

When does the next boat / ferry leave for …?	Quand part le prochain bateau / ferry pour …? kahN pahr luh pro-shaN bah-toh / fehr-ree poor
How long is the trip to …?	Combien de temps dure la traversée pour …? kohN-bee-aN duh tahn dewr lah trah-vehr-say poor

46

When do we dock in …?	**Quand est-ce qu'on accoste à …?** kahN-tes-kohN ah-kawst ah
When do we have to be on board?	**Quand devons-nous être à bord?** kahN duh-vohN-noo eh-truh ah bohr
I'd like *a first* / *an economy* class boat ticket to …	**Je voudrais un billet de bateau en** *première classe* / *classe touriste* **pour …** zhuh voo-dreh aN bee-yeh duh bah-toh ahN *prem-yehr klahss* / *klahss toor-eest* poor
I'd like …	**Je voudrais …** zhuh voo-dreh
– a single cabin.	**– une cabine individuelle.** ewn kah-been aN-dee-vee-dew-el
– a twin cabin.	**– une cabine à deux places.** ewn kah-been ah duh plahss
– an outside cabin.	**– une cabine extérieure.** ewn kah-been ex-tehr-ee-uhr
– an inside cabin.	**– une cabine intérieure.** ewn kah-been aN-tehr-ee-uhr

Aboard

I'm looking for cabin number …	**Je cherche la cabine numéro …** zhuh shehrsh lah kah-been new-meh-ro
Could I have another cabin?	**Est-ce que je pourrais changer de cabine?** es-kuh zhuh poo-reh shaN-zheh duh kah-been
Do you have anything for seasickness?	**Vous avez un remède contre le mal de mer?** voo-zah-veh aN ruh-med kohN-truh luh mahl duh mehr

Boat Trips: Additional Words

air conditioning	la climatisation
	lah klee-mah-tee-sah-see-ohN
blanket	la couverture lah koo-vehr-tewr
captain	le capitaine luh kah-pee-ten
car ferry	le car-ferry le kahr-feh-ree
coast	la côte lah koht
cruise	la croisière lah krwah-zee-ehr
deck	le pont luh pohN
deckchair	la chaise longue lah shez lohNg
dock	le point d'accostage
	luh pwahN dah-kaws-tahzh
land excursion	l'excursion f à terre
	lex-kewr-zee-ohN ah tehr
life jacket	le gilet de sauvetage
	luh gee-leh duh sohv-tahzh
life preserver	la bouée de sauvetage
	lah boo-eh duh sohv-tahzh
lifeboat	l'embarcation f de sauvetage lahN-
	bahr-kah-see-ohN duh sohv-tahzh
rough seas	la mer agitée lah mehr ah-zhee-teh
ship	le bateau luh bah-toh
shipping agency	l'agence f maritime
	lah-zhahNs mah-ree-teem
ship's doctor	le médecin de bord
	luh med-saN duh bohr
steward	le steward luh stew-ahr

Travel by Car and Motorcycle

Rental

I'd like to rent …	Je voudrais louer … zhuh voo-dreh loo-eh
– a car.	– une voiture. ewn vwah-tewr
– an automatic car.	– une voiture à embrayage automatique. ewn vwah-tewr ah ahN-bray-ahzh o-toh-mah-teek
– an off-road vehicle.	– un quatre-quatre. aN kah-truh-kah-truh
– a motorbike.	– une moto. ewn mo-toh
– an RV (recreational vehicle).	– un camping-car. aN kahN-ping-kahr
Est-ce que je pourrais voir votre permis de conduire (international)?	Could I see your (international) driver's license, please?

| I'd like to rent it for … | Je voudrais la louer pour … |
| | zhuh voo-dreh lah loo-eh poor |

– tomorrow.	– demain. duh-maN
– one day.	– une journée. ewn zhoor-nay
– two days.	– deux jours. duh zhoor
– a week.	– une semaine. ewn suh-men

| How much does that cost? | Combien ça coûte? |
| | kohN-bee-aN sah koot |

| Is mileage included? | Est-ce que le kilométrage est compris? es-kuh luh kee-low-meh-trahzh eh kohN-pree |

| Does it include fully comprehensive insurance? | L'assurance tous risques est comprise? lah-sew-rahNs too-reesk eh kohN-pree |

| Can I also return the car in …? | Je peux aussi restituer la voiture à …? zhuh puh o-see res-tee-tew-eh lah vwah-tewr ah |

| When do I have to be back by? | A quelle heure est-ce que je dois être de retour? ah kel uhr es kuh zhuh dwah eh-truh duh ruh-toor |

| Please give me a crash helmet as well. | Donnez-moi aussi un casque (de protection), s'il vous plaît. dun-nay-mwah o-see aN kahsk (duh pro-tek-see-ohN) see voo play |

info The minimum age for renting a car ranges from 21 to 25, depending on the rental company. Most rental firms require you to have a major credit card.

At the Gas / Petrol Station

Where's the nearest gas station?

Où se trouve la station-service la plus proche? oo suh troov lah stah-see-ohN-sehr-vees lah plew prawsh

Fill it up, please.

Le plein, s'il vous plaît.
luh plaN see voo play

... euros worth of ..., please.

Pour ... euro ..., s'il vous plaît.
poor ...uh-ro ... see voo play

– unleaded

– d'ordinaire sans plomb
daw-dee-nehr sahN plohN

– super unleaded

– de super sans plomb
duh sew-pehr sahN plohN

– diesel

– de gas-oil duh gah-zol

I'd like *one liter / two liters* of oil.

Je voudrais *1 litre / 2 litres* d'huile.
zhuh voo-dray *aN lee-truh / duh lee-truh* dweel

▸ *Numbers, see inside front cover*

Breakdown

I've run out of gas.

Je suis en panne sèche.
zhuh sweez-ahN pahn sesh

I've got a *flat tire / engine trouble.*

J'ai *un pneu crevé / une panne de moteur.* zheh *aN pnuh kruh-veh / ewn pahn duh mo-tuhr*

Could you give me a jump-start?

Est-ce que vous pouvez m'aider à démarrer la voiture? es-kuh voo poo-veh med-eh ah day-mah-ray lah vwah-tewr

Could you ...	Est-ce que vous pourriez ... es-kuh voo poor-ee-eh
– give me a ride?	– m'emmener un bout de chemin? mahN-muh-neh aN boo duh shuh-maN
– tow my car?	– remorquer ma voiture? ruh-maw-keh mah vwah-tewr
– send me a tow truck?	– m'envoyer la dépanneuse? mahN-vwah-yeh lah day-pahn-nuhz

Accidents

Please call ..., quick!	Vite, appelez ... veet ah-play
– an ambulance	– une ambulance! ewn ahN-bew-lahNs
– the police	– la police! lah po-leess
– the fire station	– les pompiers! lay pohN-pyeh
There's been an accident!	Il y a eu un accident! eel-yah ew aN ahk-see-dahN
... people have been (seriously) hurt.	Il y a ... blessés (graves). eel-yah ... bless-eh (grahv)
I need a first-aid kit.	J'ai besoin de pansements. zheh buh-zwahN duh pahNs-mahN
It wasn't my fault.	Ce n'est pas de ma faute. suh nay pah duh mah foht
I'd like to call the police.	Je voudrais que l'on appelle la police. zhuh voo-dray kuh lohN ah-pel lah po-leess
I had right of way.	J'avais la priorité. zhah-veh lah pree-or-ee-teh

You were tailgating.
Vous m'avez collé.
voo mah-veh kaw-lay

You were driving too fast.
Vous rouliez trop vite.
vooz roo-lee-eh tro veet

Give me your name and address, please.
Donnez-moi votre nom et votre adresse, s'il vous plaît. dun-nay-mwah vo-truh nohN eh vo-truh ah-dress see voo play

Would you act as my witness?
Vous pouvez servir de témoin?
voo poo-veh sehr-veer duh teh-mwahN

Getting Your Car Fixed

Where's the nearest garage?
Où est le garage le plus proche?
oo eh luh gah-rahzh luh plew prawsh

The car is on the road to …
La voiture est sur la route à …
lah vwah-tewr eh sewr lah root ah

Can you tow it?
Vous pouvez la remorquer?
voo poo-veh lah ruh-maw-keh

Could you have a look at it?
Vous pourriez vérifier, s'il vous plaît? voo poor-ee-eh veh-ree-fee-eh see voo play

… isn't working.
… ne marche pas. nuh mahrsh pah

Car and Motorcycle: Additional Words, page 55

My car won't start.
Ma voiture ne démarre pas.
mah vwah-tewr nuh day-mahr pah

The battery's dead.
La batterie est vide.
lah bah-teh-ree eh veed

53

The engine *sounds funny / doesn't have any power.*	Le moteur *fait un bruit bizarre / ne tire pas.* luh mo-tuhr *feh aNh brwee bee-zahr / nuh teer pah*
Can I still drive the car?	Est-ce que je peux encore rouler avec la voiture ? es-kuh zhuh puh ahN-kaw roo-lay ah-vek lah vwah-tewr
About how much will the repairs cost?	Combien va coûter la réparation, à peu près? kohN-bee-aN vah koo-teh lah ray-pah-rah-see-ohN ah puh preh
When will it be ready?	Elle sera prête quand? el suh-rah preht kahN
Do you accept coupons from the … insurance?	Vous acceptez les chèques de mon assurance multirisque …? voo zahk-sep-teh lay shek duh mohN ah-sew-rahns mewl-tee-reesk

Car and Motorcycle: Additional Words

accident insurance
le contrat multirisque de garantie automobile luh kohN-trah mewl-tee-reesk duh gah-rahN-tee oh-toh-moh-beel

accident report
le constat à l'amiable luh kohN-stah ah lah-mee-ah-bluh

air conditioning
la climatisation lah klee-mah-tee-sah-see-ohN

air filter
le filtre à air luh feel-truh ah ehr

alternator
la dynamo lah dee-nah-mo

antifreeze
l'antigel *m* lahN-tee-zhel

axle
l'essieu *m* less-yuh

battery
la batterie lah bah-tuh-ree

brake
le frein luh fraN

brake fluid
le liquide des freins luh lee-keed day fraN

brake light
le feu de stop luh fuh duh stawp

broken
cassé kah-say

bumper
le pare-chocs luh pahr-shohk

car key
la clé de la voiture lah klay duh lah vwah-tewr

car seat
le siège pour enfant luh see-ehzh poor ahN-fahN

carburetor
le carburateur luh kah-bew-rah-tuhr

catalytic converter
le pot catalytique luh poh kah-tah-lee-teek

clutch
l'embrayage *m* lahN-bray-ahzh

coolant
le liquide de refroidissement luh lee-keed duh ruh-fwah-deess-mahN

country road
la route départementale lah root day-paht-mahN-tahl

crash
le tamponnement luh tahN-pun-mahN

curve	le virage *m* luh vee-rahzh
to drive	conduire kohN-dweer
driver's license	le permis de conduire
	luh pehr-mee-duh kohN-dweer
emergency brake	le frein à main luh fraN ah maN
emergency triangle	le triangle de signalisation luh tree-
	ahN-gluh duh seen-yahl-ee-sah-see-
	ohN
engine	le moteur luh moh-tuhr
engine oil	l'huile *f* moteur lweel moh-tuhr
exhaust	le pot d'échappement
	luh poh day-shahp-mahN
expressway	l'autoroute *f* lo-toh-root
fanbelt	la courroie lah koor-wah
fender	l'aile *f* leh-luh
finish	la laque lah lahk
fire extinguisher	l'extincteur *m* lex-taNk-tuhr
first-aid kit	la boîte de premiers secours
	lah bwaht duh pruh-mee-eh suh-koor
fuse	le fusible luh few-zee-bluh
garage	le garage luh gah-rahzh
gas canister	le jerricane luh zheh-ree-kahn
gas station	la station-service
	lah stah-see-ohN-sehr-veess
gasket	le joint luh zhwaN
gear	la vitesse lah vee-tess
green insurance card	la carte verte lah kaht vehrt
headlights	le phare luh fah
heat	le chauffage luh show-fahzh
helmet	le casque luh kahsk
hood	le capot luh kah-poh
horn	le klaxon luh klahx-ohN
ignition	l'allumage *m* lah-lew-mahzh
ignition cable	le fil d'allumage
	luh feel dah-lew-mahzh

jumper cables	les câbles de démarrage lay kah-bluh duh day-mah-rahzh
kilometer	le kilomètre luh kee-low-meh-truh
light	le feu luh fuh
light bulb	l'ampoule *f* lahN-pool
luggage rack	le porte-bagages luh pawt-bah-gahzh
mirror	le miroir luh meer-wahr
motorbike	la moto lah moh-toh
multi-level parking garage	le parking couvert luh pah-king koo-vehr
neutral	le point mort luh pwaN maw
no-parking zone	l'interdiction *f* de stationner laN-tehr-deek-see-ohN duh stah-see- ohN-nay
oil change	la vidange lah vee-dahNzh
to park	se garer suh gah-ray
parking disc	le disque horaire luh deesk oh-rehr
parking lot	le parking luh pah-king
parking meter	le parcmètre luh pahk-meh-truh
radiator	le radiateur luh rah-dee-ah-tuhr
ramp	la voie d'accès à l'autoroute lah vwah dahk-say ah lo-toh-root
rear-end collision	le télescopage luh teh-leh-skoh-pahzh
rear-view mirror	le rétroviseur luh ray-tro-vee-suhr
repair	la réparation lah ray-pah-rah-see-ohN
to repair	réparer ray-pah-ray
to replace	changer shahN-zheh
right of way	la priorité lah pree-aw-ree-teh
RV (recreational vehicle)	le camping-car luh kahN-ping-kah
seatbelt	la ceinture de sécurité lah saN-tewr duh say-kew-ree-teh
service area	le relais routier luh ruh-lay roo-tyeh

shock absorber	l'amortisseur *m* lah-maw-tees-suhr
snow chains	les chaînes *f/pl* à neige
	lay shehn ah nehzh
spare tire	la roue de secours
	lah roo duh suh-koor
spark plug	la bougie lah boo-zhee
speedometer	le compteur de vitesse
	luh kohN-tuhr duh vee-tess
starter	le démarreur luh day-mah-ruhr
steering	la direction lah dee-rek-see-ohN
sunroof	le toit ouvrant luh twah oov-rahN
switch	le guichet luh ghee-sheh
tail light	les feux *m/pl* arrière
	lay fuh ah-ree-ehr
tire	le pneu luh pnuh
tire pressure	la pression des pneus
	lah pres-see-ohN day pnuh
toll	le péage luh pay-ahzh
tow rope	le câble de remorquage
	luh kah-bluh duh ruh-maw-kahzh
tow truck	la dépanneuse lah day-pahn-nuhz
transmission	la boîte de vitesses
	lah bwaht duh vee-tess
valve	la valve lah vahlv
vehicle registration	la carte grise lah kaht greez
wheel	la roue lah roo
windshield wipers	l'essuie-glace *m* less-wee glahss
wiper blades	les balais *m/pl* d'essuie-glace
	lay bah-lay dess-wee-glahss
witness	le témoin luh teh-mwahN

Public Transportation

info Subway fares are standard regardless of the distance you travel. Tickets are less expensive if you buy a book of ten (un carnet). The Paris metro closes from 12:50 am to 5:30 am.

Where's the nearest subway station?	Où est la station de métro la plus proche? oo eh lah stah-asee-ohN duh may-troh lah plew prawsh
Where's the nearest bus stop?	Où est l'arrêt d'autobus le plus proche? oo eh lah-ray-doto-bewss luh plew prawsh
Where is the bus stop to ...?	Où est l'arrêt d'autobus pour...? oo eh lah-ray doh-toh-bewss poor
Which bus / subway goes to ...?	Quel bus / Quel métro va à ...? kel bewss / kel may-tro vah ah

Le bus numéro …	The bus number …
La ligne …	The … line.
When's the next *bus* / *subway* to …?	A quelle heure part le prochain *autobus* / *métro* pour …? ah kel uhr pahr luh pro-shaN *oh-toh-bewws* / *may-tro* poor
Does this bus go to …?	Est-ce que ce bus va à …? es-kuh suh bewss vah ah
Do I have to transfer to get to …?	Pour …, est-ce que je dois changer? poor … es-kuh zhuh dwah shahN-zheh
Could you tell me where I have to *get off* / *transfer*?	Pouvez-vous me dire où je dois *descendre* / *changer*? poo-veh voo muh deer oo zhuh dwah *day-sahN-druh* / *shahN-zheh*
A ticket to …, please.	Un ticket pour …, s'il vous plaît. aN tee-keh poor … see voo play
Do you have …	Il y a … eel yah
– a one day travel pass?	– des tickets pour la journée? day tee-keh poor lah zhoor-nay
– multiple-ride tickets?	– des carnets? day kah-nay
– weekly travel passes?	– des cartes hebdomadaires? day kahrt eb-doh-mah-dehr
– a booklet of tickets?	– un carnet de tickets? aN kah-nay duh tee-keh

Numbers, see inside front cover

▶

Taking a Taxi

Could you call a taxi for me (for tomorrow morning) for … o'clock?	Vous pourriez m'appeler un taxi pour (demain à) … heures ? voo poor-ee-eh mah-play aN tahx-ee poor (duh-maN ah) … uhr
…, please.	…, s'il vous plaît. see voo play
- To the train station	– A la gare ah lah gah
- To the airport	– A l'aéroport ah lah-eh-roh-paw
- To the … Hotel	– A l'hôtel … ah loh-tel
- To the city center	– Au centre ville oh sahN-truh veel
- To … Street	– Rue … rew
How much is it to …?	Combien ce sera pour aller à …? kohN-bee-aN suh suh-rah poor ah-lay ah
Please *turn on* / *reset* the meter.	Mettez votre compteur *en marche* / *sur zéro*, s'il vous plaît. meh-teh vo-truh kohN-tuhr *ahN mahsh* / *sewr zeh-ro* see voo play
Please *wait* / *stop* here (for a moment).	*Attendez* / *Arrêtez-vous* (un instant) ici, s'il vous plaît. *ah-tahN-day* / *ah-ret-teh voo* (aN aN-stahN) ee-see see voo play
Keep the change.	Gardez la monnaie. gah-day lah mun-eh

Public Transportation and Taxi: Additional Words

bus station	la gare routière lah gah roo-tee-ehr
bus stop	l'arrêt *m* de bus lah-ray duh bewss
city center	le centre-ville luh sahN-truh veel
conductor	le contrôleur luh kohN-traw-luhr

departure	le départ luh day-pah
direction	la direction lah dee-rek-see-ohN
driver	le chauffeur luh shoh-fuhr
fare	le prix du billet luh pree dew bee-yeh
to get off	descendre day-sahN-druh
last stop	le terminus luh tehr-mee-newss
local train	le RER luh ehr-uh-ehr
schedule	l'horaire *m* loh-rehr
stop	l'arrêt *m* lah-ray
to stop	s'arrêter sah-ray-tay
taxi stand	la station de taxis
	lah stah-see-ohN duh tahx-ee
ticket	le ticket luh tee-keh
ticket machine	le distributeur automatique de
	tickets luh deess-tree-bew-tuhr
	oh-toh-mah-teek duh tee-keh
ticket validation machine	le composteur luh kohN-paws-tuhr
to transfer (train)	changer de train
	shahN-zheh duh traN
to validate	composter kohN-paws-teh

Travel
with
Children

How old is your child?
Votre enfant a quel âge?

Do you have a children's menu?
Avez-vous un menu enfant?

Frequently Asked Questions

Is there a children's discount?

Vous faites une réduction pour les enfants? voo feht ewn ray-dewk-see-ohN poor lay-zahN-fahN

How old do they have to be?

Jusqu'à / A partir de quel âge?
zhews-kah / ah pahr-teer duh kel ahzh

Tickets for two adults and two children, please.

Des billets pour deux adultes et deux enfants, s'il vous plaît. day bee-yeh poor duh-zah-dewlt eh duh-zahN-fahN see voo play

Is there a children's playground here?

Il y a un terrain de jeu pour enfants ici? eel-yah aN tehr-aN duh zhuh poor ahN-fahN ee-see

How old is your child?

Votre enfant a quel âge?
vo-truh ahN-fahN ah kel ahzh

My daughter / My son is ....

Ma fille / Mon fils a ... ans.
mah fee / mohN feess ah ... ahN

——— Travel with Children ———

Where can we buy … | Où peut-on acheter … oo puh-tohN ahsh-teh

– baby food? | – l'alimentation pour bébés? lah-lee-mahN-tah-see-ohN poor bay-bay

– children's clothes? | – les vêtements pour enfants? lay vet-mahN poor ahN-fahN

– diapers? | – les couches? lay koosh

Do you have special offers for children? | Avez-vous des promotions spéciales pour les enfants? ah-veh-voo day pro-mo-see-ohN speh-see-ahl poor lay-zahN-fahN

Have you seen a little *girl* / *boy*? | Avez-vous vu *une petite fille* / *un petit garçon*? ah-veh-voo vew *ewn puh-teet fee* / *aN puh-tee gahr-sohN*

Is there a children's section? | Il y a un compartiment pour enfants? eel-yah aN kohN-pahr-tee-mahN poor ahN-fahN

Do you have a car seat for the rental car? | Avez-vous aussi un siège pour enfants dans la voiture de location? ah-veh-voo o-see aN see-ehzh poor ahN-fahN dahN lah vwah-tewr duh loh-kah-see-ohN

Can I rent a child seat for a bicycle? | Je peux louer un siège à vélo pour enfants? zhuh puh loo-eh aN see-ehzh ah veh-lo poor ahN-fahN

Up to what age can children travel free? | Jusqu'à quel âge le trajet est gratuit pour les enfants? zhews-kah kel ahzh luh trah-zheh eh grah-twee poor lay-zahN-fahN

At the Hotel / Restaurant

Could you put in a cot?
Pourriez-vous installer un lit d'enfant? poo-ree-eh-voo aN-stah-lay aN lee dahN-fahN

Is there day care?
Peut-on faire garder les enfants? puh-tohN fehr gahr-day lay-zahN-fahN

Do you have a high chair?
Avez-vous une chaise haute pour enfants? ah-veh-voo ewn shehz oht poor ahN-fahN

Could you please warm the bottle?
Pourriez-vous réchauffer le biberon, s'il vous plaît? poor-ee-eh-voo ray-shoh-feh luh bee-buh-rohN see voo play

Do you have a children's menu?
Avez-vous un menu enfant? ah-veh voo aN muh-new ahN-fahN

Could we get half portions for the children?
Est-ce qu'on peut avoir des demies portions pour les enfants? es-kohN puh ah-vwahr day duh-mee por-see-ohN poor lay-zahN-fahN

Could we please have another place setting?
Pourrions-nous avoir un autre couvert, s'il vous plaît? poor-ee-ohN noo-zah-vwah aN o-truh koo-vehr see voo play

Swimming with Children

Is it dangerous for children?
C'est dangereux pour les enfants? say dahN-zheh-ruh poor lay-zahN-fahN

Is there a children's pool as well?	Il y a aussi un bassin pour enfants? eel-yah o-see aN bah-saN poor ahN-fahN
How deep is the water?	Quelle est la profondeur de l'eau? kel eh lah pro-fohN-duhr duh loh

Childcare and Health

Can you recommend a reliable babysitter?	Pouvez-vous nous recommander une babysitter sérieuse? poo-veh-voo noo ruh-kohN-mahN-day ewn beh-bee-sit-tehr sehr-ee-uhz
My child is allergic to milk products.	Mon enfant est allergique aux pro-duits laitiers. mohN-nahN-fahN eh ahl-lehr-zheek oh pro-dwee lay-tyeh

Health, page 175

Travel with Children: Additional Words

allergy	l'allergie f lah-lehr-zhee
baby bottle	le biberon luh bee-buh-rohN
baby phone / monitor	l'interphone m de surveillance pour bébés laN-tehr-fohn duh sewr-veh-yahNss poor bay-bay
baby powder	le talc luh tahlk
bottle warmer	le chauffe-biberon luh chohf-bee-buh-rohN
boy	le garçon luh gahr-sohN
child safety belt	la ceinture de sécurité pour enfants lah sahN-tewr duh say-kew-ree-teh poor ahN-fahN

children's portion	l'assiette *f* pour enfants
	lah-see-eht poor ahN-fahN
children's supplement	le supplément pour enfants
	luh sew-pluh-mahN poor ahN-fahN
coloring book	le livre de coloriage
	luh leev-ruh duh koh-lohr-ee-ahzh
cot	le lit d'enfant luh lee dahN-fahN
crayon	le crayon de pastel
	luh kray-ohN de pahss-tel
daughter	la fille lah fee
girl	la petite fille lah puh-teet fee
insect bite	la piqûre d'insecte
	lah pee-kewr dahN-sect
mosquito repellent	la protection contre les moustiques
	lah pro-tek-see-ohN kohN-truh lay
	moo-steek
nipple	la tétine lah teh-teen
pacifier	la sucette lah sew-set
picture book	le livre d'images pour enfants luh
	lee-vruh dee-mahzh poor ahN-fahN
playground	le terrain de jeux
	luh tehr-aN duh zhuh
playpen	le parc luh pahrk
rash	l'eczéma *m* leg-zem-ah
son	le fils luh feess
stroller	la poussette lah poo-set
toy	le jouet luh zhoo-eh
vaccination card	le carnet de vaccinations luh kahr-
	nay duh vahk-see-nah-see-ohN
visored cap	la casquette à visière
	lah kahs-ket ah vee-zee-ehr

For the Disabled

Could you open the door for me?
Vous pourriez m'ouvrir la porte?

Do you have a wheelchair I could use?
Avez-vous un fauteuil roulant pour moi?

Asking for Help

Could you help me, please?	Pouvez-vous m'aider, s'il vous plaît? poo-veh-voo med-eh see voo play
I have mobility problems.	Je suis une personne à mobilité réduite. zhuh swee ewn pehr-sun ah mo-bee-lee-teh ray-dweet
I'm disabled.	Je suis handicapé physique. zhuh swee ahn-dee-kah-pay fee-zeek
I'm visually impaired.	Je suis ♂ malvoyant / ♀ malvoyante. zhuh swee ♂ mahl-vwah-yahN / ♀ mahl-vwah-yahNt
I'm *hearing impaired* / deaf.	Je suis ♂ *malentendant* / ♀ *malentendante* / ♂ *sourd* / ♀ *sourde*. zhuh swee ♂ *mahl-ahN-tahn-dahN* / ♀ *mahl-ahN-tahn-dahNt* / ♂ *soor* / ♀ *soord*
I'm hard of hearing.	Je n'entends pas bien. zhuh nahN-tahn pah bee-aN
Could you speak up a bit, please?	Vous pourriez parler plus fort, s'il vous plaît? voo-poor-ee-eh pahr-lay plew for see voo play
Could you write that down?	Vous pouvez me l'écrire? voo poo-veh muh lay-creer
Is it suitable for wheelchair users?	Est-ce que c'est aménagé pour re-cevoir les handicapés en fauteuil roulant? es kuh say ah-men-ah-zheh poor ruh-suh-vwah lay ahN-dee-kah-pay ahN fo-tuh-yuh roo-lahN

Is there a wheelchair ramp?	Il y a une rampe pour les fauteuils roulants? eel-yah ewn rahNp poor lay fo-tuh-yuh roo-lahN
Is there a wheelchair-accessible restroom here?	Il y a des toilettes pour handicapés ici? eel-yah day twah-let poor ahN-dee-kah-pay ee-see
Can I bring my (collapsible) wheelchair?	Est-ce que je peux emmener mon fauteuil roulant (pliable)? es kuh zhuh puh ahNm-nay mohN fo-tuh-yuh roo-lahN (plee-ah-bluh)
Could you please help me get *on / off*?	Vous pourriez m'aider *à descendre / à sortir*, s'il vous plaît? voo poor-ee-eh meh-day *ah day-sahN-druh / ah saw-teer* see voo play
Could you *open / hold open* the door for me?	Vous pourriez *m'ouvrir la porte / me tenir la porte ouverte*. voo poor-ee-eh *moov-reer lah pawrt / muh tuh-neer lah pawrt oo-vehrt*
Do you have a seat where I can stretch my legs?	Avez-vous une place où je pourrais allonger les jambes? ah-veh-voo ewn plahss oo zhuh poor-eh ah-lohN-zheh lay zhahNb

At the Hotel

Does the hotel have facilities for the disabled?	L'hôtel est équipé pour recevoir les handicapés? loh-tel eh eh-kee-pay poor ruh-suh-vwah lay ahN-dee-kah-pay
Does it have a ramp for wheelchairs?	Il y a une rampe pour les fauteuils roulants? eel-yah ewn rahNp poor lay fo-tuh-yuh roo-lahN

71

Do you have a wheelchair I could use?	Avez-vous un fauteuil roulant pour moi? ah-veh voo aN fo-tuh-yuh roo-lahN poor mwah
Could you take my luggage *up to my room* / *to the taxi*?	Pouvez-vous transporter mes bagages *dans ma chambre* / *jusqu'au taxi*? poo-veh-voo trahN-spawr-teh may bah-gahzh *dahN mah shahN-bruh* / *zhews-ko tahx-ee*
Where's the nearest elevator?	Où est l'ascenseur le plus proche? oo eh lah-sahN-suhr luh plew prawsh
Could you call for me?	Pouvez-vous me composer le numéro? poo-veh-voo muh kohN-paw-say luh new-may-ro

For the Disabled: Additional Words

companion	l'accompagnateur *m* / l'accompagnatrice *f* lah-kohN-pahn-yah-tuhr / lah-kohN-pahn-yah-treess
crutch	la béquille lah bay-kee-yuh
guide dog	le chien d'aveugle luh shee-aN dah-vuh-gluh
level access	au niveau du sol oh-nee-voh dew sol
mobility cane	la canne pour nonvoyants lah kahn poor nohN-vwah-yahN
paraplegic	paraplégique pah-rah-play-zheek
suitable for the disabled	(aménagé) pour les handicapés (ah-men-ah-zheh) poor lay ahN-dee-kah-pay
wheelchair lift	la plate-forme élévatrice lah plaht-fawrm eh-lay-vah-treess
without steps	sans marches sahN mahrsh

Communications

Where can I make a phone call?
Où est-ce que je peux téléphoner?

Where's an Internet café around here?
Où y a-t-il un cybercafé ici?

Telephone

info Purchase a télécarte at the post office (La Poste), since most public phones accept only telephone cards.

▶ *Numbers, see inside front cover*

Where can I make a phone call?	**Où est-ce que je peux téléphoner?** oo es kuh zhuh puh teh-lay-fohn-eh
A (… euro) phonecard, please.	**Une carte téléphonique (à … euro), s'il vous plaît.** ewn kahrt teh-lay-fohn-eek (ah … uh-ro) see voo play
Excuse me, I need some change for the phone.	**Excusez-moi, il me faudrait des pièces pour téléphoner.** ex-kew-seh mwah eel muh fo-dreh day pee-ess poor teh-lay-fohn-eh
What's the area code for …?	**Quel est l'indicatif de …?** kel eh laN-dee-kah-teef duh
Hello? This is ….	**Allô? Je suis …** ah-loh zhuh swee
I'd like to speak to …	**Je voudrais parler à …** zhuh voo-dreh pahr-leh ah
À l'appareil.	Speaking.
Ne quittez pas.	I'll put you through.
… est en ligne en ce moment.	… is on the other line.
… n'est malheureusement pas là.	I'm afraid … isn't here.

… n'est pas là aujourd'hui.

… isn't in today.

Restez en ligne, s'il vous plaît.

Hold on, please.

Pourrais-je transmettre quelque chose?

Can I take a message?

What time does the evening rate start?

Le tarif de nuit est valable à partir de quelle heure? luh tah-reef duh nwee eh vah-lah-bluh ah pahr-teer duh kel uhr

How much is a 3-minute call to the US?

Combien coûte un appel téléphonique de trois minutes aux États-Unis? kohN-bee-aN koot aN-ah-pel teh-lay-fohn-eek duh trwah meen-ewt ohz-eh-tahs-ewn-ee

A long-distance call to …, please.

Un appel longue distance pour … s'il vous plaît. aN ah-pel lohNg dees-tahNs poor … see voo play

A collect call to …, please.

Un appel en PCV pour … s'il vous plaît. aN-ah-el ahN pay-say-vay poor … see voo play

Prenez la cabine …

Please go to booth number …

La ligne est occupée.

The line's busy.

Ça ne répond pas.

There's no reply.

Internet

Where's an internet café around here?

Où y a-t-il un cybercafé ici?
oo ee ah-teel aN see-behr-kah-feh ee-see

I'd like to send an e-mail.

Je voudrais envoyer un courriel. zhuh voo-dreh ahN-vwah-yeh aN koor-ee-el

Which computer can I use?

Quel ordinateur est-ce que je peux utiliser? kel aw-deen-ah-tuhr es-kuh zhuh puh ew-tee-lee-zeh

How much is it for 15 minutes?

Combien coûte quinze minutes?
kohN-bee-aN koot kaNz meen-ewt

Could you help me, please?

Pourriez-vous m'aider?
poor-ee-eh-voo med-eh

E-mail

annuler	Logout
boîte f de réception	Inbox
brouillons m/pl	Draft
composer	Compose
corbeille f	Trash
envoyer	Send
imprimer	Print
messages m/pl envoyés	Outbox / Sent mail
répondre	Reply
répondre à tous	Reply all
retour	Back
sauvegarder	Save
supprimer	Delete
transférer	Forward

Eating and Drinking

The menu, please.
La carte, s'il vous plaît.

The bill, please.
L'addition, s'il vous plaît.

Reservations

Is there ... around here?

Où y a-t-il ici ... oo ee ah-teel ee-see

– a café

– un salon de thé?
aN sah-lohN duh teh

– a bar

– un bistrot? aN bees-troh

– a reasonably priced restaurant

– un restaurant pas trop cher?
aN rest-o-rahN pah tro shehr

A table for ..., please.

Une table pour ... personnes, s'il vous plaît. ewn tah-bluh poor ... pehr-sun see voo play

I'd like to reserve a table for *two* / *six* people for ... o'clock.

Je voudrais réserver une table pour *deux* / *six* personnes pour ... heures. zhuh voo-dreh ray-zehr-veh ewn tah-bluh poor *duh* / *seess* pehr-sohn poor ... uhr

We've reserved a table for ... people (in the name of ...)

Nous avons réservé une table pour ... personnes (au nom de ...). noo-zah-vohN ray-zehr-veh ewn tab-luh poor ... pehr-sun (oh nohN duh)

Is this *table* / *seat* free?

Est-ce que cette *table* / *place* est libre? es kuh set *tah-bluh* / *plahss* eh lee-bruh

Excuse me, where are the restrooms?

Pardon, où sont les toilettes?
pahr-dohN oo sohN lay twah-let

En zone fumeurs ou non-fumeurs?

Smoking or non-smoking (area)?

info Places where you can eat: Auberge – An inn, often in the country; serves full meals and drinks. Bistrot – Selling mostly drinks and basic food (sandwiches, salads, snacks) with traditional French cuisine; usually not very expensive. Brasserie – A large café serving good, simple food and drinks, very often offering a plat du jour (dish of the day). Buffet – A restaurant found in large train stations; the food is generally good. Café / Bar – Serves coffee and drinks, sometimes light meals, too. Crêperie – Offers snacks of light pancakes with various fillings. Restaurant – Rated by scores of professional and amateur gourmets. Restoroute – A large restaurant just off a highway (motorway); table or cafeteria service is available. Rôtisserie – Specializes in meat products: roast chickens, quiches, sausages, ham, hors-d'œuvre, etc. Routier – Roughly equivalent to a roadside diner; the food is simple but can be surprisingly good.

Menu

LE MENU DU PETIT DÉJEUNER

Breakfast Menu

café *m*	kah-feh	coffee
café *m* au lait	kah-feh oh lay	coffee with milk
café *m* crème	kah-feh krem	coffee with foamed milk
chocolat *m* chaud	sho-ko-lah sho	hot chocolate
croissant *m*	krwah-sahN	croissant
œuf *m*, œufs *pl*	uhf uhf	egg / eggs
œuf *m* brouillé	uhf broo-yeh	scrambled eggs
œuf *m* dur	uhf dewr	hard-boiled egg
œuf *m* à la coque	uhf ah lah kawk	soft boiled egg
thé *m*	teh	tea
thé *m* au citron	teh oh see-trohN	tea with lemon

MENU

POTAGES ET SOUPES

Soups

bouillabaisse *f*	boo-yah-bess	fish soup from southern France
consommé *m*	kohN-so-may	clear broth
soupe *f* à l'oignon gratinée	soup ah lohN-yohN grah-tee-nay	onion soup, oven-browned with croutons and cheese
soupe *f* de poisson	soup duh pwah-sohN	fish soup

HORS-D'ŒUVRE

Cold Appetizers

aspic *m* d'anguille
ah-speek dahN-gwee-yuh
jellied eel

avocat *m* vinaigrette
ah-vo-kah veen-eh-gret
avocado in vinaigrette sauce

charcuterie *f* shahr-kew-tree
cold cut platter

cœurs *m/pl* d'artichauts
kuhr dahr-tee-sho
artichoke hearts

crevettes *f/pl* kruh-vet
shrimp

crudités *f/pl* (variées)
krew-dee-teh (vah-ree-eh)
dish of raw vegetables and fruit

foie *m* gras fwah-grah
pâté de foie gras

huîtres *f/pl* we-truh
oysters

jambon *m* blanc
zhahN-bohN blahN
cooked ham

jambon *m* cru
zhaN-bohN krew
uncooked ham

jambon *m* fumé
zhaN-bohN few-may
smoked ham

melon *m* muh lohN
melon

pâté *m* pah-teh
pâté or meat pie

pâté *m* de foie gras en croûte pah-teh duh fwah grah ahN croot
pâté de foie gras wrapped in dough

pâté *m* de foie haché fin
pah-teh duh fwah ah-sheh faN
liverwurst pâté

pissenlits *m/pl* au lard
pee-sahN-lee oh-lahr
dandelion salad with bacon

quiche *f* lorraine
keesh law-ren
quiche with egg, cheese, and bacon

rillettes *f/pl* ree-yet — potted, finely chopped pork
salade *f* de concombres — cucumber salad
sah-lahd duh kohN-kohN-bruh
salade *f* de tomates — tomato salad
sah-lahd duh toh-maht
salade *f* mixte — mixed salad
sah-lahd meext
salade *f* niçoise — green salad with
sah-lahd nee-swahz — tomatoes, eggs,
anchovies and olives

saucisson *m* de campagne — liverwurst
so-see-sohN duh kahN-pahn-yuh
saumon *m* fumé — smoked salmon
so-mohN few-may
terrine *f* de canard — pâté / meat pie made of
teh-reen duh kah-nahr — roast duck
terrine *f* du chef — pâté / home made meat
teh-reen duh shef — pie

ENTRÉES

Hot Appetizers / Snacks

croque-monsieur *m* — toasted ham and cheese
krawk-muh-syuhr
crêpes *f/pl* krehp — very thin pancakes
escargots *m/pl* es-kahr-go — snails
omelette *f* awm-let — omelette
omelette *f* au lard — omelette with bacon
awm-let oh lahr
omelette *f* aux champignons — omelette with mushrooms
awm-let oh sham-peen-yohN
omelette *f* nature — plain omelette
awm-let nah-tewr

VIANDES

Meat Dishes

agneau *m* ahn-yo	lamb
andouillette *f* ahN-doo-yet	fried sausage made of tripe
bifteck *m* beef-tek	steak
bœuf *m* bourguignon buhf boor-geen-yohN	beef stew in red wine
bœuf *m* mode buhf mode	pot roast
bœuf *m* buhf	beef
boudin *m* noir boo-daN nwahr	blood sausage
cassoulet *m* kahss-oo-leh	beef, sausage and bean stew
côte *f* kawt	pork chops
escalope *f* panée es-kah-lawp pah-nay	breaded veal
filet *m* de bœuf fee-lay duh buhf	fillet of beef
gigot *m* d'agneau zhee-go dahn-yo	leg of lamb
grillade *f* gree-yahd	mixed grill
jarret *m* de veau zhah-reh duh vo	knuckle of veal
lièvre *m* lee-eh-vruh	wild hare
mouton *m* moo-tohN	mutton
paupiette *f* (de veau) po-pyet duh vo	slices of rolled and braised veal
pieds *m/pl* de cochon pee-yeh duh ko-shohN	pig's feet
quenelles *f/pl* kuh-nel	dumplings made from either meat or fish

ris *m* de veau ree duh vo	sweetbread
rôti *m* ro-tee	roast
sauté *m* de veau	ragout made of veal
so-teh duh vo	
selle *f* d'agneau	saddle of lamb
sell dahn-yo	
steak *m* au poivre	pepper steak
steak oh pwahv-ruh	
steak *m* haché	meat loaf
steak ahsh-eh	
tournedos *m* toor-nuh-doh	fillet steak
veau *m* vo	veal

GIBIER

Game

cerf *m* sehr	venison
civet *m* de marcassin	young wild boar in wine
see-veh duh mahr-kah-saN	sauce
médaillons *m/pl* de	medallions of venison
chevreuil	
may-dah-yohN duh shev-ruh-yuh	
sanglier *m* sahN-glee-eh	wild boar

VOLAILLE

Poultry

blanc *m* de poulet	chicken breast
blahN duh poo-leh	
canard *m* à l'orange	duck braised with
kah-nahr ah law-rahNzh	oranges and orange
	liqueur

confit m de canard   pieces of duck, potted in
kohN-fee duh kah-nahr   its own fat
coq m au vin   kawk oh vaN   chicken in red or white
    wine sauce

pintade f   paN-tahd   guinea fowl
poulet m rôti   poo-lay ro-tee   broiled chicken

POISSONS

Fish

anguille f   ahN-gwee-yuh   eel
brandade f   brahN-dahd   dried cod, mashed and
    cooked, prepared with
    cream, olive oil and garlic

brochet m   braw-sheh   pike
cabillaud m   kah-bee-yoh   cod
calmars m/pl frits   fried squid rings
kahl-mahr free
carpe f   kahrp   carp
colin m   ko-laN   hake (salt water fish,
    similar to a codfish)

églefin m   ehg-luh-faN   haddock
friture f   free-tewr   fried fish
hareng m saur   ahr-ahN sor   bloater, smoked herring
lotte f   lawt   monkfish
morue f   maw-rew   dried cod
rouget m   roo-zheh   barbel (salt water fish
    with firm and lean meat)

saumon m   so-mohN   salmon
sole f   sawl   sole
thon m   tohN   tuna
truite f   trweet   trout

truite *f* au bleu
trweet oh bluh

poached trout

truite *f* aux amandes et au
beurre noir   trweet oh-zah-
mahNd eh oh buhr nwahr

trout with almonds and
browned butter

truite *f* meunière
trweet muhn-yehr

trout turned in flour and
fried

turbot *m*   tew-boh

turbot

COQUILLAGES ET CRUSTACÉS

Seafood

coquilles *f/pl* Saint-Jacques
ko-kee saN-zhahk

scallops

crabe *m*   krahb

crab

crevette *f*   kruh-vet

shrimp, prawn

écrevisses *f/pl*   eh-kruh-veess

fresh water crabs

homard *m* à l'armoricaine
oh-mahr ah lahr-mor-ee-ken

lobster in white wine
sauce

huîtres *f/pl*   wee-truh

oysters

langouste *f*   lahN-goost

rock lobster

langoustines *f/pl*
lahN-goos-teen

scampi

moules *f/pl* frites   mool freet

mussels with French fries

plateau *m* de fruits de mer
plah-toh duh frwee duh mehr

seafood platter

GARNITURES

Side Dishes

pâtes *f/pl*   paht

noodles

pommes *f/pl* de terre
pum duh tehr

potatoes

pommes *f/pl* de terre sautées pum duh tehr so-teh	home fries
pommes *f/pl* de terre vapeur pum duh tehr vah-puhr	boiled potatoes
pommes *f/pl* frites pum freet	French fries
riz *m* ree	rice

LÉGUMES

Vegetables and Legumes

artichauts *m/pl* ahr-tee-sho	artichokes
asperges *f/pl* ahs-pehrzh	asparagus
aubergines *f/pl* o-behr-zheen	eggplants
carottes *f/pl* kah-rawt	carrots
champignons *m/pl* shahN-peen-yohN	mushrooms
champignons *m/pl* de Paris shaN-peen-yohN duh pah-ree	button mushrooms
chou *m* fleur shoo fluhr	cauliflower
chou *m* rave shoo rahv	cabbage with large fleshy edible stem
chou *m* rouge shoo roozh	red cabbage
choucroute *f* shoo-croot	sauerkraut
choux *m/pl* de Bruxelles shoo duh brewx-el	Brussels sprouts
courgettes *f/pl* koor-zhet	zucchini
endives *f/pl* ahN-deev	endives
épinards *m/pl* eh-pee-nahr	spinach
fenouil *m* fuh-noo-yuh	fennel

gratin *m* dauphinois grah-taN doh-feen-wah	oven-browned potatoes
haricots *m/pl* blancs ah-ree-koh blahN	white beans
haricots *m/pl* verts ah-ree-koh vehr	green beans
macédoine *f* de légumes mah-seh-dwahn duh lay-gewm	mixed vegetables
navets *m/pl* nah-veh	turnips
petits pois *m/pl* puh-tee pwah	peas
poivron *m* pwah-vrohN	bell peppers
ratatouille *f* rah-tah-too-yuh	vegetable dish with tomatoes, peppers, eggplant etc.

LE MODE DE PRÉPARATION
Ways of Cooking

à la broche ah lah brawsh	spit-roasted, on a skewer
(cuit) à la vapeur (kwee) ah lah vah-puhr	steamed
à l'étuvé ah lay-tew-veh	steamed
bien cuit bee-aN kwee	well-done
cuit au four kwee oh foor	baked
cuit à l'eau kwee ah lo	boiled
flambé flahN-bay	flambé
fumé few-may	smoked
gratiné grah-tee-nay	oven-browned
grillé gree-eh	grilled
(fait) maison (feh) may-zohN	homemade

pané   pah-nay   breaded
rôti   ro-tee   roasted

FROMAGES

Cheese

bleu *m*   bluh   blue cheese
doux   doo   mild
fromage *m*   fro-mahzh   cheese
fromage *m* au lait cru   raw-milk cheese
fro-mahzh oh lay crew
fromage *m* de brebis   feta cheese
fro-mahzh duh breh-bee
fromage *m* de chèvre   goat cheese
fro-mahzh duh chehv-ruh
plateau *m* de fromages   cheese platter
plah-toh duh fro-mahzh

DESSERTS

Desserts

beignets *m/pl* aux pommes   apple fritters
ben-yeh oh pum
charlotte *f*   shahr-lawt   charlotte (made from
                                   vanilla cream and
                                   ladyfingers soaked in
                                   liqueur)

clafoutis *m* aux cerises   dessert made with
clahfoo-tee oh suh-reez   cherries and batter
coupe *f* maison   sundae (of the house)
koop may-zohN

crème *f* caramel krem kah-rah-mel	crème caramel
flan *m* flahN	flan
glace *f* glahss	ice cream
glace *f* au chocolat glahss oh sho-ko-lah	chocolate ice cream
glace *f* à la fraise glahss ah lah frehz	strawberry ice cream
glace *f* à la vanille glahss ah lah vah-nee-yuh	vanilla ice cream
île *f* flottante eel floh-tahNt	merengue in custard
macédoine *f* de fruits mah-seh-dwahn duh frwee	fruit salad
meringue *f* mehr-aNg	merengue
parfait *m* pahr-feh	parfait, soft ice cream

FRUITS

Fruit

dattes *f/pl* daht	dates
figues *f/pl* feeg	figs
fraises *f/pl* frehz	strawberries
framboises *f/pl* frahN-bwahz	raspberries
pastèque *f* pahs-tek	watermelon
pêche *f* pehsh	peach
poire *f* pwahr	pear
pomme *f* pum	apple
raisin *m* ray-saN	grapes

GÂTEAUX ET PÂTISSERIES

Sweets and Pastries

baba *m* au rhum bah-bah oh rohm	yeast cake soaked in rum
chausson *m* aux pommes shos-sohN oh pohm	apple turnover
chou *m* à la crème shoo ah lah krem	cream puff
éclair *m* eh-klehr	long cake with a cream filling
mille-feuille *m* meel-fuh-yuh	Danish pastry with cream small cream puffs
profiteroles *f/pl* pro-fee-teh-rawl	cream puffs with chocolate or mocha cream
tarte *f* Tatin tahrt tahtaN	apple cake with caramel icing
tarte *f* aux fraises tahrt oh frehz	strawberry tarts
tuiles *f/pl* aux amandes tweel o-zah-mahnd	almond cookies

LISTE DES CONSOMMATIONS

Beverages

APÉRITIFS
Aperitifs

kir *m* keer	white wine with blackcurrant liqueur

kir *m* royal   keer rwah-yahl   champagne with black-
currant liqueur

pastis *m*   pahs-teess   anisette-flavored liqueur

Vins

Wine

brut   brew   dry (champagne)

champagne *m*   champagne
shaN-pahn-yuh

cuvée *f* du patron   house wine
kew-veh dew pah-trohN

(demi-)sec   duh-mee sek   (medium) dry

doux   doo   sweet

porto *m*   paw-toh   port

vin *m* blanc   vaN blahN   white wine

vin *m* de pays   locally-produced wine
vaN duh pay-ee

vin *m* de table   table wine
vaN duh tah-bluh

vin *m* d'appellation   high-quality wine
contrôlée   vaN dah-pel-ah-
see-ohN kohN-tro-lay

vin *m* mousseux   sparkling wine
vaN moos-suh

vin *m* rosé   vaN ro-zeh   rosé wine

vin *m* rouge   vaN roozh   red wine

── Eating and Drinking ──

AUTRES BOISSONS ALCOOLISÉES

Other Alcoholic Beverages

bière *f* bee-yehr	beer
bière *f* blonde	lager beer
bee-yehr blohNd	
bière *f* brune	dark beer
bee-yehr brewn	
bière *f* pression	draft beer
bee-yehr pres-see-ohN	
bière *f* sans alcool	non-alcoholic beer
bee-yehr sahN ahl-kawl	
calvados *m* kahl-vah-dawss	apple brandy
cassis *m* kah-seess	blackcurrant liqueur
cidre *m* see-druh	hard cider
digestif *m* dee-zhes-teef	digestive (brandy)
eau-de-vie *f* oh-duh-vee	spirits
marc *m* mahr	grappa, marc

BOISSONS NON ALCOOLISÉES

Non-alcoholic Beverages

citron *m* pressé	freshly squeezed lemon
see-trohN pres-say	juice
eau *f* minérale	mineral water
oh meen-eh-rahl	
eau *f* minérale gazeuse	carbonated mineral water
oh meen-eh-rahl gah-zuhz	
eau *f* minérale non gazeuse	non-carbonated
oh meen-eh-rahl nohN gah-zuhz	mineral water
grenadine *f* gruh-nah-deen	drink made from
	pomegranate syrup

jus *m* zhew   juice
jus *m* de pomme   apple juice
zhew duh pum
jus *m* d'orange   orange juice
zhew daw-rahNzh
limonade *f* lee-mo-nahd   lemonade
menthe *f* mahNt   peppermint syrup with
                                   water

BOISSONS CHAUDES

Hot Beverages

café *m* kah-feh   coffee
café *m* au lait   coffee with milk
kah-feh oh leh
café *m* crème kah-feh krem   coffee with foamed milk
café *m* express   espresso
kah-feh es-press
chocolat *m* chaud   hot chocolate
sho-ko-lah sho
infusion *f* aN-few-zee-ohN   herbal tea
infusion *f* de tilleul   linden blossom tea
aN-few-zee-ohN duh tee-uhl
thé *m* teh   tea
thé *m* au citron   tea with lemon
teh oh see-trohN
thé *m* au lait teh oh leh   tea with milk

Ordering

The menu, please.
La carte, s'il vous plaît.
lah kahrt see voo play

info When asking for the waiter you say Monsieur! or, for the waitress, Mademoiselle!

I'd just like a snack.
Je voudrais seulement manger un petit quelque chose. zhuh voo-dray suhl-mahN mahN-zheh aN puh-tee kel-kuh shoze

Are you still serving hot meals?
Est-ce qu'on peut encore avoir quelque chose de chaud à manger? es kohN puh ahN-kaw ah-vwah kel-kuh shoze duh sho ah mahN-zheh

I'd just like something to drink.
Je voudrais seulement boire quelque chose. zhuh voo-dray suhl-mahN bwahr kel-kuh shoze

Are you still serving food?
Vous servez encore à manger ?
voo sehr-veh ahN-kaw ah mahN-zheh

What do you recommend?
Que me recommandez-vous?
kuh muh ruh-koh-mahN-day-voo

Que désirez-vous boire?
What would you like to drink?

Do you sell wine by the glass?
Avez-vous aussi du vin en carafe?
ah-veh voo o-see dew vaN ahN kah-rahf

I'll have …	Je voudrais … zhuh voo-dray
– a glass of red wine.	– un verre de vin rouge. aN vehr duh vaN roozh
– a bottle of white wine.	– une bouteille de vin blanc. ewn boo-teh-yuh duh vaN blahN
– a carafe of house wine.	– une carafe de vin de la maison. ewn kah-rahf duh vaN duh lah may-zohN
– a beer.	– une bière. ewn bee-yehr
– a pitcher of water.	– une carafe d'eau. ewn kah-rahf doh
– some more bread.	– encore un peu de pain. ahN-kaw aN puh duh paN
– a *small* / *large* bottle of mineral water.	– une *petite* / *grande* bouteille d'eau minérale. ewn *puh-teet* / *grahNd* boo-teh-yuh doh meen-eh-rahl
– a cup of coffee.	– une tasse de café. ewn tahss duh kah-feh
Que désirez-vous manger?	What would you like to eat?
I'll have …	Je voudrais … zhuh voo-dray
– the … euro menu.	– le menu à … euros. luh muh-new ah … uh-roh
– a portion of …	– une portion de … ewn paw-see-ohN duh
– a piece of …	– une part de … ewn pahr duh
What's today's special?	Quel est le plat du jour? kel eh luh plah dew zhoor
What are the regional specialities here?	Quelles sont les spécialités de la région? kel sohN lay speh-see-ah-lee-teh duh lah ray-zhee-ohN

Do you serve …

Avez-vous … ah-veh-voo

– diabetic meals?

– des plats pour diabétiques?
day plah poor dee-ah-bay-teek

– dietary meals?

– des plats de régime?
day plah duh ray-zheem

– vegetarian dishes?

– des plats végétariens?
day plah veh-zheh-tah-ree-aN

Does it have … in it?
I'm not allowed to eat
any.

Est-ce qu'il y a … dans ce plat? Je
n'ai pas le droit d'en manger. es
keel ya … dahN suh plah zhuh nay pah
luh drwah dahN mahN-zheh

Without … for me,
please.

Pour moi sans …, s'il vous plaît.
poor mwah sahN … see voo play

Comme *entrée /
dessert*, qu'est-ce que
vous prenez?

What would you like *as an appetizer /
for dessert*?

I won't have *an appe-
tizer / a dessert*, thank
you.

Merci, je ne prends pas *d'entrée /
de dessert*. mehr-see zhuh nuh prahN
pah *dahN-treh / duh des-sehr*

Could I have … instead
of …?

Est-ce que je pourrais avoir … au
lieu de …? es kuh zhuh poor-eh ah-
vwah … oh lyuh duh

Comment désirez-
vous votre steak?

How would you like your steak?

Rare.

Saignant. sen-yahN

Medium.

A point. ah pwahN

Well done.

Bien cuit. bee-aN kwee

Complaints

That's not what I ordered. I wanted …	Ce n'est pas ce que j'ai commandé. Je voulais … suh neh pah suh kuh zheh kohN-mahN-day zhuh voo-lay
Have you forgotten my …?	Avez-vous oubliez ♂ mon / ♀ ma …? ah-veh-voo oo-blee-eh mohN / mah
There's / There are no …	Il n'y a pas de… eel nee ah pah duh
The food is *cold / too salty.*	Le repas est *froid / trop salé.* luh ruh-pah eh *frwah / tro sah-lay*
The meat isn't cooked through.	La viande n'est pas assez cuite. lah vee-ahNd neh pah-zah-say kweet
The meat's very tough.	La viande est dure. lah vee-ahNd eh dewr
Please take it back.	Remportez cela, s'il vous plaît. rahN-paw-teh suh-lah see voo play

► *Expressing Likes and Dislikes, page 19*

Paying

► *Numbers, see inside front cover*

| The bill, please. | L'addition, s'il vous plaît. lah-dee-see-ohN see voo play |
| I'd like a receipt, please. | J'aimerais bien un reçu, s'il vous plaît. zhem-ehr-eh bee-aN aN ruh-sew see voo play |

We'd like to pay separately.	Nous voudrions payer séparément. noo voo-dree-ohN pay-yeh say-pahr-eh-mahN
All together, please.	Une seule addition, s'il vous plaît. ewn suhl ah-dee-see-ohN see voo play
Vous êtes satisfait(s)?	Did you enjoy it?

Expressing Likes and Dislikes, page 19

Please give my compliments to the chef.	Mes compliments au chef de cuisine. may kohN-plee mahN oh shef duh kwee-zeen
I think there's been a mistake.	A mon avis, il y a une erreur. ah mohN ah-vee eel yah ewn eh-ruhr

info Service is generally included in the bill but if you are happy with the service a personal tip is appreciated—round the bill up 1-2 euros.

Having Lunch / Dinner Together

Enjoy your meal!	Bon appétit! bohN-nah-peh-tee
Cheers!	Santé! sahN-teh
Vous aimez ça?	Are you enjoying your meal?
It's very nice, thank you.	Merci, c'est très bon. mehr-see say treh bohN
Encore un peu de ...?	Would you like some more ...?
Yes, please.	Oui, volontiers. wee vol-ahN-tyeh

No thank you, I'm full.	Je n'ai plus faim, merci. zhuh nay plew faN mehr-see
What's that?	Qu'est-ce que c'est? kes kuh say
Could you pass me the ..., please?	Vous pourriez me passer ..., s'il vous plaît? voo poor-ee-eh muh pahss-say... see voo play
Do you mind if I smoke?	Ça vous dérange si je fume? sah voo day-rahNzh see zhuh fewm
Thank you very much for the invitation.	Merci pour l'invitation. mehr-see poor laN-vee-tah-see-ohN
It was excellent.	C'était excellent. say-teh ex-say-lahN

Eating and Drinking: Additional Words

appetizer	l'entrée *f* lahN-treh
ashtray	le cendrier luh sahN-dree-yeh
bar	le bistrot luh beess-tro
bottle	la bouteille lah boo-teh-yuh
bread	le pain luh paN
butter	le beurre luh buhr
chair	la chaise lah shez
cold	froid frwah
complete meal	le menu luh muh-new
course	le plat luh plah
cover charge	le couvert luh koo-vehr
cup	la tasse lah tahss
diet	le régime luh ray-zheem
dinner	le dîner luh dee-nay
dressing	la vinaigrette lah vee-neh-gret
drink	la boisson lah bwahs-sohN
fatty	gras *f*, grasse, *pl* grah grahss
fish bone	l'arête *f* lah-ret

— Eating and Drinking —

food	le repas luh ruh-pah
fork	la fourchette lah foor-shet
fresh	frais *f*, fraîche, *pl* freh fresh
fruit	les fruits *m/pl* lay frwee
garlic	l'ail *m* lie
glass	le verre luh vehr
gravy	la sauce lah sohss
homemade	(fait) maison (feh) may-zohN
hot	chaud sho
hot (spicy)	épicé eh-pees-say
jam	la confiture lah koN-fee-tewr
ketchup	le ketchup luh ketch-up
knife	le couteau luh koo-toh
lean	maigre meh-gruh
light food	la cuisine diététique lah kwee-zeen dee-eh-teh-teek
lunch	le déjeuner luh day-zhuh-nay
main course	le plat de résistance luh plah duh ray-zees-tahNs
margarine	la margarine lah mahr-gahr-een
mayonnaise	la mayonnaise lah mah-yun-nez
meal	le plat *m* luh plah
mustard	la moutarde lah moo-tahrd
napkin	la serviette lah sehr-vyet
oil	l'huile *f* lweel
pasta	pâtes *f/pl* paht
(ground) pepper	le poivre luh pwahv-ruh
piece	le morceau luh maw-so
plate	l'assiette *f* lahs-syet
portion	la portion lah paw-see-ohN
potatoes	pommes *f/pl* de terre pum duh tehr
raw	cru crew
restaurant	le restaurant luh rest-o-rahN
rice	riz *m* ree

roll	le petit pain luh puh-tee paN
salad	salade *f* sah-lahd
salt	le sel luh sel
sandwich	le sandwich luh sahN-dweetch
sauce	la sauce lah sohss
seasoned	assaisonné ah-say-zohN-nay
service	le service luh sehr-veess
side dish	la garniture lah gahr-nee-tewr
silverware	les couverts *m/pl* lay koo-vehr
soup	le potage luh po-tahzh
sour	aigre eh-gruh
(sparkling / non-sparkling) mineral water	l'eau *f* minérale (gazeuse / non-gazeuse) lo mee-nay-rahl (gah-zuhz / nohN-gah-zuhz)
specialty	la spécialité lah speh-see-ah-lee-teh
spoon	la cuillère lah kwee-yehr
sugar	le sucre luh sew-kruh
sweet	sucré sew-cray
sweetener	la saccharine lah sahk-ah-reen
table	la table lah tah-bluh
tea	thé *m* teh
tip	le pourboire luh poor-bwahr
toothpick	le cure-dents luh kewr-dahN
vegetables (raw)	les crudités *f/pl* lay crew-dee-teh
vegetarian	végétarien veh-zheh-tah-ree-aN
vinegar	le vinaigre luh veen-eh-gruh
Waiter / Waitress	Monsieur / Mademoiselle moN-seeyew / mahd-mwah-sell
yogurt	le yaourt luh yah-oor

▶ *More Food Items, page 110*

Shopping

I'm just looking, thanks.
Merci, je regarde seulement.

How much is that?
Ça coûte combien?

Paying

How much is that?	**Ça coûte combien?** sah koot kohN-bee-aN
How much *is / are* …?	**Combien *coûte / coûtent* …?** kohN-bee-aN *koot / koot*
That's too expensive.	**C'est trop cher pour moi.** say tro shehr poor mwah
Can you come down a little?	**Vous pouvez faire quelque chose pour le prix?** voo poo-veh fehr kel-kuh shoze poor luh pree
Do I get a discount if I pay cash?	**Vous me faites une réduction, si je paie en liquide?** voo muh fet ewn ray-dewk-see-ohN see zhuh pay ahN lee-keed
Do you have anything on sale?	**Vous avez des offres spéciales?** voo-zah-veh day-zawf-fruh spay-see-ahl
Can I pay with this credit card?	**Je peux payer avec (cette) carte de crédit?** zhuh puh pay-yeh ah-vek (set) kahrt duh kray-dee
I'd like a receipt, please.	**J'aimerais avoir une facture.** zhem-eh-reh ah-vwahr ewn fahk-tewr

General Requests

Where can I get …?	**Où est-ce que je peux acheter …?** oo es kuh zhuh puh ahsh-teh
Vous désirez?	What would you like?
Je peux vous aider?	Can I help you?

I'm just looking, thanks.	Merci, je regarde seulement. mehr-see zhuh ruh-gahrd suhl-mahN
I'm being helped, thanks.	Merci, on me sert. mehr-see ohN me sehr
I'd like …	Je voudrais … zhuh voo-dreh
Je regrette, nous n'avons plus de …	I'm afraid we've run out of …
I don't like that so much.	Cela ne me plaît pas tellement. suh-lah nuh muh play pah tel-mahN
Is there anything else you could show me?	Vous pourriez me montrer autre chose? voo poo-ree-eh muh mohN-tray o-truh shoze
I'll have to think about it.	Je dois encore réfléchir. zhuh dwah ahN-kaw ray-fleh-sheer
I like that. I'll take it.	Cela me plaît. Je le prends. suh-lah muh play zhuh luh prahN
Vous désirez encore quelque chose?	Anything else?
That's all, thanks.	Merci, ce sera tout. mehr-see suh suh-rah too
Do you have a bag?	Vous auriez un sac? voo-zo-ree-eh aN sahk
Could you wrap it up as a present, please?	Vous pourriez me faire un paquet cadeau? voo poo-ree-eh muh fehr aN pah-keh kah-doh
I'd like to *exchange / return* this.	Je voudrais *échanger / rendre* cela. zhuh voo-dray *eh-shahN-zheh / rahN-druh* suh-lah

105

General Requests: Additional Words

(too) big	(trop) grand (tro) grahN
bigger	plus grand plew grahN
cheap(er)	(moins) cher (mwahN) shehr
check	le chèque luh shek
credit card	la carte de crédit lah kahrt duh kray-dee
end of season sales	les soldes *f/pl* lay sawld
(too) expensive	(trop) cher (tro) shehr
money	l'argent *m* lahr-zhahN
on sale	l'article *m* en promotion lahr-tee-kluh ahN pro-mo-see-ohN
receipt	le reçu luh ruh-sew
sale	les soldes *f/pl* lay sawld
self-service	le libre service luh lee-bruh sehr-veess
to buy	acheter ahsh-teh
to cost	coûter koo-teh
to return	rendre rahN-druh
to show	montrer mohN-tray
window display	la vitrine lah vee-treen

Shops and Stores

info Stores in France are generally open Monday through Saturday from 9 am to 7 pm. Some stores are closed during lunchtime, from 12-2 pm, except department stores or supermarkets. Most stores are closed on Sundays, some on Mondays as well.

antique shop	le magasin d'antiquités
	luh mah-gah-zaN dahN-tee-kee-teh
bakery	la boulangerie
	lah boo-lahN-zheh-ree
bookstore	la librairie lah lee-breh-ree
boutique	la boutique lah boo-teek
butcher's	la boucherie lah-boosh-uh-ree
candy store	la confiserie lah kohN-fee-suh-ree
chemist	la droguerie la drawg-uh-ree
delicatessen	l'épicerie f fine lay-pee-suh-ree feen
	le grand magasin
department store	luh grahN mah-gah-zaN
dry cleaner's	le pressing luh pres-sing
electronics store	le magasin d'électroménager
	luh mah-gah-zaN day-lek-tro-may-nah-zheh
fish store	la poissonnerie lay pwah-sun-uh-ree
florist	le fleuriste luh fluhr-eest
grocery store	l'épicerie f lay-pee-suh-ree
hairdresser	le coiffeur luh kwah-fur
hardware store	la quincaillerie lah kaN-kigh-uh-ree
jeweler's	le bijoutier luh bee-zhoo-tyeh
kiosk	le kiosque luh kee-awsk
laundromat	la laverie automatique
	lah lah-veh-ree o-toh-mah-teek

leather goods store	la maroquinerie
	lah mah-raw-keen-uh-ree
market	le marché luh mahr-sheh
music store	le magasin de musique
	luh mah-gah-zaN duh mew-zeek
newsstand	le marchand de journaux
	luh mahr-shahN duh zhoor-no
optician	l'opticien m lawp-tee-see-aN
pastry shop	la pâtisserie lah pah-tee-suh-ree
perfume shop	la parfumerie lah pah-few-muh-ree
pharmacy	la pharmacie lah fahr-mah-see
photo shop	le magasin d'articles photographiques luh mah-gah-zaN dahr-tee-kluh fo-toh-grah-feek
shoe repair shop	le cordonnier luh kaw-dohN-yeh
shoe store	le magasin de chaussures
	luh mah-gah-zaN duh sho-sewr
shopping center	le centre commercial
	luh sahN-truh kohN-mehr-see-ahl
souvenir shop	le magasin de souvenirs
	luh mah-gah-saN duh soo-ven-eer
sporting goods store	le magasin d'articles de sport luh mah-gah-zaN dahr-tee-kluh duh spawr
stationery store	la papeterie lah pahp-eh-tree
supermarket	le supermarché
	luh sew-pehr-mahr-sheh
tobacconist	le bureau de tabac
	luh bew-ro duh tah-bah
watch shop	l'horloger law-lo-zheh

Food

What's that?	Qu'est-ce que c'est? kes kuh say
Please give me …	Donnez-moi …, s'il vous plaît. dun-nay-mwah… see voo-play
– 100 grams (.022 lb) of …	– cent grammes de … sahN grahm duh
– a kilo (2.2 lbs) of …	– un kilo de … aN kee-lo duh
– a liter of …	– un litre de … aN lee-truh duh
– half a liter of …	– un demi-litre de … aN duh-mee lee-truh duh
– four slices of …	– quatre tranches de … kah-truh trahNsh duh
– a piece of …	– un morceau de … aN maw-so duh
A little *less* / *more*, please.	Un peu *moins* / *plus*, s'il vous plaît. aN puh *mwahN* / *plew* see voo play
Could I try some?	J'aimerais bien en essayer, s'il vous plaît? zhem-eh-reh bee-aN ahN es-eh-yeh see voo play

Food: Additional Words

alcohol-free beer	la bière sans alcool
	lah bee-yehr sahN-zahl-kawl
apple	la pomme lah pum
apple cider (alcoholic)	le cidre luh see-druh
apple juice	le jus de pomme luh zhew duh pum
apricot	l'abricot *m* lahb-ree-ko
artichoke	l'artichaut *m* lahr-tee-sho
asparagus	l'asperge *f* lah-spehrzh
avocado	l'avocat *m* lah-vo-kah
baby food	les aliments *m/pl* pour bébés
	lay-zah-lee-mahN poor bay-bay
balsamic vinegar	le vinaigre balsamique
	luh vee-nehg-ruh bahl-sah-meek
banana	la banane lah bah-nahn
basil	le basilic luh bah-see-leek
beans	les haricots *m/pl* lay ah-ree-ko
beef	le bœuf luh buhf
beer	la bière lah bee-yehr
bell pepper	le poivron luh pwah-vrohN
boiled ham	le jambon cuit luh zhahN-bohN kwee
bread	le pain luh paN
broccoli	le brocoli luh braw-kaw-lee
butter	le beurre luh buhr
cabbage	le chou luh shoo
cake	le gâteau luh gah-to
canned foods	les conserves *f/pl* lay kohN-sehrv
canned sardines	les sardines *f/pl* à l'huile
	lay sahr-deen ah lweel
carrots	les carottes *f/pl* lay kah-rawt
cereal	le muesli luh mews-lee
cheese	le fromage luh fro-mahzh
cherries	les cerises *f/pl* lay suh-reez
chicken	le poulet luh poo-lay

110

chicory	l'endive *f* lahN-deev
chili pepper	le piment luh pee-mahN
chives	les ciboulettes lay see-boo-let
chocolate	le chocolat luh sho-ko-lah
pork / lamb chop	la côtelette de porc / d'agneau lah kawt-uh-let duh pawr / dah-nyo
cocoa	le cacao luh kah-cow
coffee	le café luh kah-feh
cold cuts	la charcuterie lah shahr-kew-teh-ree
cookies	les biscuits *m/pl* lay beess-kwee
corn	le maïs luh mah-eess
cream	la crème lah krem
cucumber	le concombre luh kohN-kohN-bruh
(veal) cutlet	l'escalope *f* (de veau) less-kah-lawp (duh vo)
egg	l'œuf *m*, les œufs *pl* luhf, lay-zuh
eggplant	l'aubergine *f* lo-behr-zheen
fish	le poisson luh pwahs-sohN
fruit	les fruits *m/pl* lay frwee
garlic	l'ail *m* ligh
grapes	les raisins *m/pl* lay ray-saN
green beans	les haricots *m/pl* verts lay ah-ree-ko vehr
ground meat	la viande hachée lah vee-yahNd ash-eh
ham	le jambon luh zhahN-bohN
herbal tea	l'infusion *f* laN-few-zee-ohN
herbs	les fines herbes *f/pl* lay feen-zehrb
honey	le miel luh mee-yel
ice cream	la glace lah glahss
jam	la confiture lah kohN-fee-tewr
juice	le jus luh zhew
ketchup	le ketchup luh ketch-up
kiwi	le kiwi luh kee-vee
lamb	l'agneau *m* lahn-yo

leek	**le poireau** luh pwah-ro
lemon	**le citron** luh see-trohN
lettuce	**la salade** lah sah-lahd
liver pâté	**le pâté de foie** luh pah-teh duh fwah
lowfat milk	**le lait demi-écrémé** luh lay duh-mee eh-kray-may
margarine	**la margarine** lah mah-gah-reen
marmalade	**la marmalade à l'orange** la mahr-mah-lahd ah law-rahNzh
mayonnaise	**la mayonnaise** la mah-yuh-nez
meat	**la viande** lah vee-ahNd
melon	**le melon** luh muh-lohN
milk	**le lait** luh lay
mushrooms	**les champignons** *m/pl* lay shaN-peen-yohN
nectarine	**la nectarine** lah nek-tah-reen
nuts	**les noix** *f/pl* lay nwah
oil	**l'huile** *f* lweel
olive oil	**l'huile d'olive** lweel doh-leev
olives	**les olives** *f/pl* lay-zo-leev
onion	**l'oignon** *m* lohN-yohN
orange	**l'orange** *f* law-rahNzh
orange juice	**le jus d'orange** luh zhew daw-rahNzh
oregano	**l'origan** *m* law-ree-gahn
oysters	**les huîtres** *f/pl* lay weet-ruh
paprika	**le piment** luh pee-mahN
parsley	**le persil** luh pehr-see
pasta	**les pâtes** *f/pl* lay paht
peach	**la pêche** lah pehsh
peanuts	**les cacahuètes** *f/pl* lay kah-kah-wet
pear	**la poire** lah pwahr
peas	**les petits pois** *m/pl* lay puh-tee pwah
(ground) pepper	**le poivre** luh pwah-vruh

pepperoni	le salami luh sah-lah-mee
pickles	les cornichons *m/pl* lay kaw-nee-shohN
pineapple	l'ananas *m* lah-nah-nah
plums	les prunes *f/pl* lay prewn
pork	le porc luh pawr
potatoes	les pommes *f/pl* de terre lay pum duh tehr
poultry	la volaille lah vol-igh-yuh
raspberries	les framboises *f/pl* lay frahN-bwahz
red wine	le vin rouge luh vaN roozh
rice	le riz luh ree
roll	les petits pains *m/pl* lay puh-tee paN
rolled oats	les flocons *m/pl* d'avoine lay flaw-kohN dah-vwahn
rosemary	le romarin luh ro-mah-raN
rye bread	le pain noir luh paN nwahr
salt	le sel luh sel
sausages	la saucisse lah so-seess
semolina	la semoule lah suh-mool
smoked ham	le jambon cru luh zhahN-bohN krew
soda	la limonade lah lee-mo-nahd
sparkling / non- sparkling mineral water	l'eau *f* minérale *gazeuse / non* *gazeuse* lo meen-eh-rahl gah-zuhz / nohN gah-zuhz
spices	les épices *f/pl* lay-zeh-peess
spinach	les épinards *m/pl* lay-zeh-pee-nahr
steak	le steak luh steak
strawberries	les fraises *f/pl* lay frez
sugar	le sucre luh sew-kruh
sweetener	la saccharine la sahk-ah-reen
tarragon	l'estragon *m* less-trah-gohN
tea	le thé luh teh
teabag	le sachet de thé luh sah-sheh duh teh

thyme	le thym luh taN
tomato	la tomate lah toh-maht
tuna	le thon luh tohN
veal	le veau luh vo
veal filet	l'escalope *f* less-kah-lawp
vegetables	les légumes *m/pl* lay lay-gewm
vinegar	le vinaigre luh vee-nehg-ruh
watermelon	la pastèque lah pahss-tek
white beans	les haricots *m/pl* blancs lay ah-ree-ko blahN
white bread	le pain blanc luh paN blahN
white wine	le vin blanc luh vaN blahN
whole grain bread	le pain complet luh paN kohN-pleh
wine	le vin luh vaN
without preservatives	sans agents *m/pl* de conservation sahN ah-zhahn duh kohN-sehr-vah- see-ohN
yogurt	le yaourt luh yah-oor
zucchini	la courgette lah koor-zhet

Souvenirs

'd like …	Je voudrais … zhuh voo-dray
– a nice souvenir.	– un joli souvenir. aN zho-lee soo-ven-eer
– a present.	– un cadeau. aN kah-do
– something typical of the region.	– quelque chose de typique de la région. kel-kuh shoze duh tee-peek duh lah ray-zhee-ohN
Is this handmade?	Est-ce que c'est fait main? es-kuh say feh-maN
Is this *antique /* *genuine*?	Est-ce que c'est *ancien / du vrai*? es kuh say *ahN-see-aN / dew vreh*

Souvenirs: Additional Words

antique	l'antiquité *f* lahN-teek-kee-teh
arts and crafts	l'artisanat *m* lahr-tee-sahn-ah
belt	la ceinture lah saN-tewr
beret	le béret (basque) luh bay-ray (bahsk)
blanket	la couverture lah koo-vehr-tewr
bowl (salad)	le saladier luh sah-lahd-yeh
bowl	le bol luh bawl
certificate	le certificat luh sehr tee-fee-kah
crockery, tableware	la vaisselle lah veh-sel
cup, goblet	le gobelet luh gawb-lay
cup, mug	la tasse la tahss
hand-carved	sculpté à la main scewlp-teh ah lah maN
handmade	fait à la main feh ah maN
handpainted	peint à la main paN ah lah maN
jewelry	les bijoux *m/pl* lay bee-zhoo
jug	le broc luh brawk

115

lace	la dentelle lah dahN-tel
lavender	la lavande la lah-vahNd
leather	le cuir luh kweer
pottery	la poterie lah paw-tuh-ree
pottery, ceramics	la céramique la seh-rah-meek
purse, handbag	le sac à main luh sahk ah maN
silk scarf	le foulard en soie luh foo-lahr ahN swah
souvenir	le souvenir luh soo-ven-eer
special blend of herbs from the Provence region	les herbes *f/pl* de Provence lay-zehrb duh pro-vahNs
stoneware	la faïence lah figh-yahNs
tablecloth	la nappe la nahp
terracotta	la terre cuite la tehr kweet
vase	le vase luh vahz

Clothing

Buying Clothes

I'm looking for …	Je cherche … zhuh shehrsh
Quelle est votre taille?	What size are you?
I'm (US) size …	Ma taille (américaine) est … mah tigh-yuh (ah-meh-ree-ken) eh

info

	Dresses/Suits						Shirts			
American	8	10	12	14	16	18	15	16	17	18
British	10	12	14	16	18	20				
Continental	38	40	42	44	46	48	38	41	43	45

Do you have it in a size …?	Est-ce que vous l'avez aussi dans la taille…? es kuh voo lah-veh o-see dahN lah tigh-yuh…
Do you have it in a different color?	Est-ce que vous l'avez aussi dans une autre couleur? es kuh voo lah-veh o-see dahN-zewn o-truh koo-luhr

Colors, page 119

Could I try this on?	Je peux l'essayer? zhuh puh less-eh-yeh
Where is there a mirror?	Où est le miroir? oo eh luh meer-wahr
Where are the fitting rooms?	Où sont les cabines d'essayage? oo sohN lay kah-been dess-eh-yahzh

117

What fabric is this?	**C'est quoi comme tissu?** say kwah kom tees-sew
It doesn't fit me.	**Cela ne me va pas.** suh-lah nuh muh vah pah
It's too *big* / *small*.	**C'est trop *grand* / *petit*.** say tro grahN / puh-tee
It fits nicely.	**Cela va parfaitement.** suh-lah vah pahr-fet-mahN

Laundry and Dry Cleaning

I'd like this dry-cleaned.	**Je voudrais faire nettoyer cela.** zhuh voo-dreh fehr net-twah-yeh suh-lah
Could you remove this stain?	**Vous pouvez enlever cette tache?** voo poo-veh ahN-luh-vay set tahsh
When can I pick it up?	**Quand est-ce que je peux venir le reprendre?** kahN-tes kuh zhuh puh ven-eer luh ruh-pahN-druh

Fabrics and Materials

camel hair	**le poil de chameau** luh pwahl duh shah-mo
cashmere	**le cachemire** luh kahsh-meer
cotton	**le coton** luh koh-tohN
fleece	**la fibre polaire** la fee-bruh po-lehr
lambswool	**le mohair** luh mo-hehr
leather	**le cuir** luh kweer
linen	**le lin** luh laN
man-made fiber	**le synthétique** luh saN-teh-teek
microfiber	**la microfibre** lah mee-kro-fee-bruh

natural fiber	les fibres *f/pl* naturelles
	lay fee-bruh nah-tewr-el
pure new wool	la pure laine vierge
	lah pewr len vee-yerzh
silk	la soie la swah
suede	le chamois luh shah-mwah
wool	la laine lah len

Colors

beige	beige behzh
black	noir nwahr
blue	bleu bluh
brown	marron mah-rohN
burgundy	rouge foncé roozh fohN-say
colorful	multicolore mewl-tee-ko-lawr
golden	doré daw-ray
gray	gris gree
green	vert vehr
light blue	bleu ciel bluh see-yel
navy blue	bleu marine bluh mah-reen
pink	rose rohz
purple	violet vee-o-lay
red	rouge roozh
silver	argent ahr-zhahN
solid-color	uni ew-nee
turquoise	turquoise tewr-kwahz
white	blanc *m*, blanche *f* blahN blahnsh
yellow	jaune zhone

Clothing: Additional Words

anorak	l'anorak *m* lah-naw-rahk
bathing suit	le maillot de bain
	luh ma-yoh duh baN
bathrobe	le peignoir (de bain)
	luh pen-ywahr (duh baN)
beach hat	le chapeau de soleil
	luh shah-po-duh so-lay
belt	la ceinture lah san-tewr
bikini	le bikini luh bee-kee-nee
blazer	le blazer luh blah-zehr
blouse	le chemisier luh shuh-mee-zee-yeh
bra	le soutien-gorge
	luh soo-tee-aN gawrzh
briefs	le slip luh sleep
cap	le bonnet luh bun-eh
coat	le manteau luh mahN-toh

dress	la robe lah rawb
gloves	les gants *m/pl* lay gahN
hat	le chapeau luh shah-po
jacket	la veste lah vest
jeans	le jean luh jean
long	long lohN
long sleeves	les manches *f/pl* longues
	lay mahNsh lohNg
pajamas	le pyjama luh pee-dzhah-mah
panties	la culotte lah kew-lawt
pants	le pantalon luh pahN-tah-lohN
pantyhose	le collant luh ko-lahN
raincoat	l'imperméable *m*
	laN-pehr-may-ah-bluh
scarf	l'écharpe *f* lay-shahrp
shirt	la chemise lah shmeez
short	court koor
short sleeves	les manches courtes *f/pl*
	lay mahNsh koort
shorts	le short luh shawr
skirt	la jupe lah jewp
socks	les chaussettes *f/pl* lay sho-set
sports jacket	le veston luh ves-tohN
stockings	les mi-bas *m/pl* lay mee-bah
suit	le costume luh kaw-stewm
suit	le tailleur luh ta-yuhr
sweater	le pullover luh pewl-oh-vehr
swimming trunks	le caleçon de bain
	luh kahl-sohN duh baN
T-shirt	le T-shirt luh tee shert
tie	la cravate lah krah-vaht
track pants	le pantalon de jogging
	luh pahN-tah-lohN duh zhawg-ing
tracksuit	la tenue de jogging
	lah tuh-new duh zhawg-ing

undershirt	le maillot de corps
	luh mah-yot duh kawr
underwear	les dessous *m/pl* lay des-soo
vest	le gilet luh zhee-lay
wrinkle-free	infroissable aN-frwah-sah-bluh
zipper	la fermeture éclaire
	lah fehr-meh-tewr eh-klehr

In the Shoe Store

I'd like a pair of …	Je voudrais une paire de …
	zhuh voo-dreh ewn pehr duh
Quelle est votre pointure?	What's your shoe size?
I wear size …	Je porte du … zhuh pawrt dew
The heels are too *high* / *low*.	Le talon est trop *haut* / *plat*.
	luh tah-lohN eh tro *oh* / *plah*
They're too *big* / *small*.	Elles sont trop *grandes* / *petites*.
	el sohN tro *grahNd* / *puh-teet*
They're tight around here.	Elles me serrent ici.
	el muh sehr ee-see

info

	Women's Shoes				Men's Shoes							
American	6	7	8	9	6	7	8	8½	9	9½	10	11
British	4½	5½	6½	7½								
Continental	37	38	39	40	38	39	40	41	42	43	44	44

Shoe Store: Additional Words

boots	les bottes *f/pl* lay bawt
flip-flops	les sandales *f/pl* de bain
	lay sahN-dahl duh baN
high heels	les escarpins *m/pl*
	lay-zess-kahr-paN
hiking boots	les chaussures *f/pl* de montagne
	lay sho-sewr duh mohN-tahn-yuh
insoles	les semelles *f/pl* lay suh-mel
leather	le cuir luh kweer
leather sole	la semelle en cuir
	la suh-mel ahN kweer
rubber boots	les bottes *f/pl* en caoutchouc
	lay bawt ahN kah-oo-kshoo
sandals	les sandales *f/pl* lay sahN-dahl
shoe polish	le cirage luh see-rahzh
shoelaces	les lacets *m/pl* lay lah-say
shoes	les chaussures *f/pl* lay sho-sewr
size	la pointure lah pwaN-tewr
sneakers	les baskets *m/pl* lay bahs-keh
suede	le chamois luh shah-mwah
tight	serré sehr-ray
walking shoes	les chaussures *f/pl* de randonnée
	lay sho-sewr duh rahN-dun-eh

Jewelry and Watches

I need a new battery for my watch.	J'ai besoin d'une pile neuve pour cette montre. zhay buh-swaN dewn peel nuhv poor set mohN-truh

I'm looking for a nice souvenir / present.	Je cherche un joli *souvenir / cadeau.* zhuh shehrsh aN zho-lee *soo-ven-eer / kah-doh*
Dans quel prix?	How much do you want to spend?
What's this made of?	C'est en quoi? say ahN kwah

Jewelry and Watches: Additional Words

alarm clock	le réveil luh ray-veh
bracelet	le bracelet luh brahss-lay
brooch	la broche lah brawsh
carat	le carat luh kah-rah
clip-on earrings	les boucles *f/pl* d'oreille à clips lay boo-kluh daw-ray ah kleep
costume jewelry	le bijou fantaisie luh bee-zhoo fahN-teh-zee
diamond	le diamant luh dee-ah-mahN
earrings	les boucles *f/pl* d'oreille lay boo-kluh daw-ray
gold	l'or *m* lawr
gold-plated	doré daw-ray
jewelry	les bijoux *m/pl* lay bee-zhoo
necklace	la chaîne lah shen
pearl	la perle lah pehrl
pendant	le pendentif luh pahN-dahN-teef
platinum	le platine luh plah-teen
ring	la bague lah bahg
silver	l'argent *m* lah-zhahN
watch	la montre lah mohN-truh
watchband	le bracelet de montre luh brahss-lay duh mohN-truh

Health and Beauty

adhesive bandage	le pansement adhésif
	luh pahNs-mahN ah-day-seef
baby powder	la poudre pour bébés
	lah poo-druh poor bay-bay
barrette	la barrette lah bah-ret
blush	le blush luh blush
body lotion	la lotion corporelle
	lah lo-see-ohN kor-por-el
brush	la brosse lah brawss
comb	le peigne luh pen-yuh
condoms	les préservatifs *m/pl*
	lay pray-sehr-vah-teef
cotton balls	le coton luh co-tohN
cotton swabs	les Cotons-Tiges® *m/pl*
	lay co-tohN-teeg
dental floss	le fil dentaire luh feel dahN-tehr
deodorant	le déodorant luh day oh-daw-rahN
detergent	le détergent luh day-tehr-zhahN
(elastic) hairband	l'élastique *m* à cheveux
	lay-lahs-teek ah shuh-vuh
eye shadow	l'ombre *f* à paupières
	lohN-bruh ah po-pyehr
eyeliner	le crayon khôl luh cray-ohN kohl
face wash	le lait démaquillant
	luh lay day-mah-kee-yahN
fragrance-free	non parfumé nohN pahr-few-may
hairclips	les pinces *f/pl* à cheveux
	lay paNs ah shuh-vuh
hairspray	la laque à cheveux
	lah lahk ah shuh-vuh
hand cream	la crème de soins pour mains
	lah krem duh swan poor maN

125

hypoallergenic	**hypoallergènique** ee-poh-ahl-ehr-zheh-neek
lip balm	**le stick à lèvres** luh steek ah leh-vruh
lipstick	**le rouge à lèvres** luh roozh ah leh-vruh
mascara	**le rimmel** luh ree-mel
mirror	**le miroir** luh meer-wahr
moisturizer	**la crème de jour** lah krem duh zhoor
mosquito repellent	**la protection anti-moustiques** lah pro-tek-see-ohN ahN-tee-moo-steek
mousse	**la mousse renforçatrice** lah mooss rahN-faw-sah-treess
nail file	**la lime à ongles** lah leem ah ohN-gluh
nail polish	**le vernis à ongles** luh vehr-nee ah ohN-gluh
nail polish remover	**le dissolvant** luh dee-sawl-vahN
nail scissors	**les ciseaux** *m/pl* **à ongles** lay see-zo ah ohN-gluh
nailbrush	**la brosse à ongles** lah brawss ah ohN-gluh
night cream	**la crème de nuit** lah krem duh nwee
perfume	**le parfum** luh pahr-faN
razor blade	**la lame de rasoir** lah lahm duh rah-swah
sanitary napkins	**les serviettes** *f/pl* **hygiéniques** lay sehrv-yet hee-zhen-eek
shampoo	**le shampooing** luh shahN-pwaN
shaving cream	**la mousse à raser** lah mooss ah rah-zeh
shower gel	**le gel douche** luh zhel doosh
soap	**le savon** luh sah-vohN
styling gel	**le gel coiffant** luh zhel kwah-fahN
sun protection factor (SPF)	**le facteur de protection solaire** luh fahk-tuhr duh pro-tek-see-ohN so-lehr
sunscreen	**la crème solaire** lah krem so-lehr

126

suntan lotion	le lait solaire luh lay so-lehr
tampons	les tampons *m/pl* lay tahN-pohN
tissues	les mouchoirs *m/pl* en papier lay moosh-wahr ahN pah-pyeh
toilet paper	le papier hygiénique luh pah-pyeh hee-zhen-eek
toothbrush	la brosse à dents lah brawss ah dahN
toothpaste	le dentifrice luh dahN-tee-freess
toothpicks	le cure-dents luh kewr-dahN
tweezers	la pince à épiler lah paNs ah eh-pee-lay
washcloth	le gant de toilette luh gahN duh twah-let
wipes	les lingettes *f/pl* lay laN-zhet

Household Articles

aluminum foil	l'aluminium *m* ménager lahl-meen-yum may-nah-zheh
bottle opener	le décapsuleur luh day kahp-sewl-uhr
broom	le balai luh bah-lay
bucket	le seau luh soh
can opener	l'ouvre-boîte *m* loo-vruh bwaht
candles	les bougies *f* lay boo-zhee
charcoal	le charbon de bois luh shahr-bohN duh bwah
cleaning products	les produits *m/pl* de nettoyage lay pro-dwee duh net-wah-yazh
cloth	le chiffon luh shee-fohN
clothes pins	les pinces *f/pl* à linge lay paNs ah laNzh
cooler	la glacière la glah-syehr
corkscrew	le tire-bouchon luh teer-boo-shohN
cup	la tasse lah tahss

127

detergent	la lessive lah les-seev
dishtowel	la lavette lah lah-vet
dishwashing detergent	le liquide vaisselle
	luh lee-keed veh-sel
fork	la fourchette lah foor-shet
frying pan	la poêle lah pwahl
glass	le verre luh vehr
grill lighter	l'allume-feu m lahl-ewm-fuh
insect spray	le spray anti-insectes
	luh spreh ahN-tee aN-sekt
knife	le couteau luh koo-to
laundry line	la corde à linge lah kord ah laNzh
light bulb	l'ampoule f lahN-pool
lighter	le briquet luh bree-keh
matches	les allumettes f/pl lay-zahl-ew-met
methylated spirits	l'alcool m à brûler
	lahl-kawl ah brew-lay
mosquito coil	la spirale anti-moustiques
	lah spee-rahl ahN-tee-moo-steek
napkins	les serviettes f/pl lay sehr-vyet
paper towels	le rouleau de papier (absorbant)
	luh roo-lo duh pah-pyeh (ahb-sawr-bahN)
plastic cup	le gobelet en plastique
	luh gawb-lay ahN plah-steek
plastic plate	l'assiette f en plastique
	lahs-syet ahN plah-steek
plastic utensils	les couverts m/pl en plastique
	lay koo-vehr ahN plah-steek
plastic wrap	le film fraîcheur luh feelm freh-shuhr
plate	l'assiette f lah-syet
pocket knife	le couteau de poche
	luh koo-toh duh pawsh
safety pin	l'épingle f de sûreté
	lay-paN-gluh duh sewr-teh

saucepan	la casserole lah kahss-rawl
scissors	les ciseaux *m/pl* lay see-zo
sewing needle	l'aiguille *f* à coudre
	lay-gwee ah koo-druh
sewing thread	le fil à coudre luh feel ah koo-druh
spoon	la cuillère lah kwee-yehr
stain remover	le détachant luh day-tahsh-mahN

Electrical Articles

adapter	l'adaptateur *m* lah-dahp-tah-tuhr
alarm clock	le réveil luh ray-veh
battery	la pile lah peel
extension cord	la rallonge lah rah-lohNzh
flashlight	la lampe de poche
	lah lahNp duh pawsh
immersion heater	le thermoplongeur
	luh tehr-mo-plohN-zhuhr
pocket calculator	la calculette lah kahl-kew-let
razor	le rasoir luh rah-swah

At the Optician

My glasses are broken.	Mes lunettes sont cassées.
	may lew-net sohN kah-say
Can you repair this?	Pouvez-vous réparer cela?
	poo-veh voo ray-pah-ray suh-lah
I'd like some disposable lenses.	J'aimerais avoir des lentilles journalières jetables. zhem-eh-reh ah-vwahr day lahN-tee-yuh zhoor-nahl-yehr zhuh-tah-bluh

Avez-vous un carnet pour *les lunettes* / *lentilles*?	Do you have a *glasses* / *contact lens* prescription card?
Combien de dioptries avez-vous?	What's your prescription?
I've got … dioptres in the left eye and … dioptres in the right.	J'ai … dioptries à gauche et … dioptries à droite. zheh … dee-awp-tree ah gosh eh … dee-awp-tree ah drwaht
I've *lost* / *broken* a contact lens.	J'ai *perdu* / *cassé* une lentille (de contact). zheh *pehr-dew* / *kah-say* ewn lahN-tee-yuh (duh kohN-tahkt)
I need some saline solution for *hard* / *soft* contact lenses.	Il me faudrait une solution de conservation pour lentilles *dures* / *souples*. eel muh fo-dreh ewn so-lew-see-ohN duh kohN-sehr-vah-see-ohN poor lahN-tee-yuh *dewr* / *soo-pluh*
I need some cleaning solution for *hard* / *soft* contact lenses.	Il me faudrait une solution de nettoyage pour lentilles *dures* / *souples*. eel muh fo-dreh ewn so-lew-see-ohN duh net-twah-yahzh poor lahN-tee-yuh *dewr* / *soo-pluh*
I'd like a pair of sunglasses.	Je voudrais des lunettes de soleil. zhuh voo-dreh day lew-net duh so-lay

At the Photo Store

I'd like …	Je voudrais … zhuh-voo-dreh
– a memory card for this camera.	– une carte mémoire pour cet appareil. ewn kahrt mehm-wahr poor set ahp-pah-ray
– film for this camera.	– une pellicule pour cet appareil. ewn pel-ee-cewl poor set ahp-pah-ray
– color film.	– un film (négatif en couleurs). aN feelm (nay-gah-teef ahN koo-luhr)
– slide film.	– une pellicule pour diapositives. ewn pel-ee-kewl poor dee-ah-pos-ee-teev
– 24 / 36-exposure film.	– une pellicule de vingt-quatre / trente-six expositions. ewn pel-lee-kewl duh vaNt-kah-truh / trahNt-seess ex-po-zee-see-ohN
I'd like some batteries for this camera.	Je voudrais des piles pour cet appareil. zhuh voo-dreh day peel poor set ahp-pah-ray
Could you put the film in for me, please?	Vous pouvez me placer la pellicule dans l'appareil, s'il vous plaît? voo-poo-veh muh plah-say lah pel-ee-kewl dahN lah-pah-ray see voo play
When will the prints be ready?	Les photos seront prêtes quand? lay fo-toh suh-rohN pret kahN
Can you repair my camera?	Vous pouvez réparer mon appareil photo? voo poo-veh ray-pah-ray mohN ahp-pah-ray fo-toh
It won't advance.	Il bloque. eel blawk

The shutter release / *The flash* doesn't work.	*Le déclencheur / Le flash* ne fonctionne pas. *luh day-clahN-shuhr / luh flahsh* nuh fohNk-see-on pah
I'd like to have some passport photos taken.	Je voudrais faire faire des photos d'identité. zhuh voo-dreh fehr fehr day fo-toh dee-dahN-tee-teh

Photo Store: Additional Words

camcorder	le caméscope luh kahm-eh-skawkp
CD / DVD	le *CD / DVD* luh *say-day / day-veh-day*
digital camera	l'appareil *m* photo numérique lah-pah-ray fo-toh new-mehr-eek
exposure meter	le posemètre luh pohs-meh-truh
(film) speed	la sensibilité lah saN-see-bee-lee-teh
film camera	la caméra lah kah-meh-rah
filter	le filtre luh feel-truh
flash	le flash luh flahsh
lens	l'objectif *m* lawb-zhek-teef
negative	le négatif luh nay-gah-teef
photo	la photo la fo-toh
self-timer	le déclencheur automatique luh day-klahN-shuhr o-toh-mah-teek
SLR camera	le réflex luh ray-flex
telephoto lens	le téléobjectif luh teh-lay-awb-zhek-teef
UV filter	le filtre UV luh feel-truh ew-veh
video camera	la caméra vidéo lah kahm-eh-rah vee-day-o
video cassette	la vidéocassette lah vee-day-o-kahs-set
wide-angle lens	l'objectif *m* grand angle lawb-zhek-teef grahn-than-gluh
zoom lens	le zoom luh zoom

At the Music Store

Do you have any CDs by ...?

Vous avez des CDs de ...?
voo-zah-veh day say-day duh

I'd like a CD of traditional French music.

J'aimerais bien un CD de musique française *traditionelle / folklorique*.
zhem-eh-reh bee-aN aN say-day duh mew-zeek frahN-seh-zhuh *trah-dee-see-ohN-el / fawlk-law-reek*

Music: Additional Words

cassette	la cassette lah kah-set
headphones	les écouteurs lay-zeh-koo-tuhr
music	la musique lah mew-zeek
radio	la radio lah rah-dee-oh
Walkman®	le baladeur luh bah-lah-duhr

Books and Stationery

I'd like ...

Je voudrais ... zhuh voo-dreh

- an American newspaper.

– un journal américain.
  aN zhoor-nahl ah-may-ree-kaN

- an American magazine.

– un magazine américain.
  aN mah-gah-zeen ah-may-ree-kaN

- a map of the area.

– une carte de la région.
  ewn kahrt duh lah ray-zhee-ohN

- a map of the town.

– un plan de la ville.
  aN plahN duh lah veel

Do you have a more recent paper?

Vous auriez aussi un journal plus récent? voo-zo-ree-eh oh-see aN zhoor-nahl plew ray-sahN

133

Do you have any English books?	Est-ce que vous avez des livres anglais? es-kuh voo-zah-veh day lee-vruh ahN-gleh

Books and Stationery: Additional Words

ballpoint pen	le stylo bille luh stee-lo beel
cookbook	le livre de cuisine luh lee-vruh duh kwee-zeen
detective novel	le policier luh paw-lee-see-eh
dictionary	le dictionnaire luh deek-see-ohN-nehr
envelope	l'enveloppe f lahN-vel-awp
eraser	la gomme lah gawm
felt tip	le feutre luh fuh-truh
glue	la colle lah cawl
hiking map	la carte de randonnées pédestres lah kahrt duh rahN-dun-eh pay-des-truh
magazine	le magazine illustré m luh mah-gah-zeen ee-lew-stray
map of cycling routes	la carte de randonnées cyclistes lah kahrt duh rahN-dun-eh see-kleest
novel	le roman luh ro-mahN
paper	le papier luh pahp-yeh
pencil	le crayon luh cray-ohN
pencil sharpener	le taille-crayon luh tigh-cray-ohN
playing cards	les cartes f/pl à jouer lay kahrt ah zhoo-eh
postcard	la carte postale lah kahrt pos-tahl
printer cartridge	la cartouche d'imprimante lah kahr-toosh daN-pree-mahNt
road map	la carte routière lah kahrt roo-tyehr

travel guide	**le guide de voyage**
	luh geed duh vwah-ahzh
tape	**le ruban adhésif**
	luh rew-bahN ahd-eh-seef
writing pad	**le bloc-notes** luh blawk-noht
writing paper	**le papier à lettres**
	luh pahp-yeh ah leh-truh

At the Tobacco Shop

A pack of cigarettes *with / without* filters, please.

Un paquet de cigarettes *avec / sans* filtres, s'il vous plaît. aN pah-keh duh see-gah-ret *ah-vek / sahN* feel-truh see voo play

A *pack / carton* of ..., please.

Un paquet / Une cartouche de ..., s'il vous plaît. *aN pah-keh / ewn kahr-toosh* duh... see voo play

Are these cigarettes *strong / mild*?

Ces cigarettes sont *fortes / légères*? say see-gah-ret sohN *fawrt / lay-zhehr*

A pouch of *pipe / cigarette* tobacco, please.

Un paquet de tabac *pour pipe / à cigarettes*, s'il vous plaît. aN pah-keh duh tah-bah *poor peep / ah see-gah-ret* see voo play

Could I have a *lighter / book of matches*, please?

Un briquet / Une boîte d'allumettes, s'il vous plaît. *aN bree-keh / ewn bwaht dahl-ewm-et* see voo play

135

Tobacco: Additional Words

cigarillos	les cigarillos *m/pl* lay see-gah-ree-yo
cigars	les cigares *m/pl* llay see-gahr
pipe	la pipe lah peep
pipe cleaner	le cure-pipe luh kewr-peep

Sports and Leisure

How do we get to the beach?
Comment va-t-on à la plage?

I'd like to rent a bicycle.
Je voudrais louer un vélo.

Activities

Beach and Pool

How do we get to the beach?

Comment va-t-on à la plage?
kohN-mahN vah-tohN ah lah plahzh

Is swimming permitted here?

On peut se baigner ici?
ohN puh suh ben-yeh ee-see

Are there (strong) currents around here?

Y a-t'il des courants (forts) ici?
ee-ah-teel day- koo-rahN (fawr) ee-see

When is *low / high* tide?

Quelle est l'heure de la marée *basse / haute*? kel eh luhr duh lah mah-ray *bahss / oht*

Are there jellyfish around here?

Est-ce qu'il y a des méduses ici?
es keel ya day may-dews ee-see

I'd like to rent …

Je voudrais louer …
zhuh voo-dreh loo-eh

– a deckchair.

– une chaise longue.
ewn shehz lohNg

– an umbrella.
– a boat.

– un parasol. aN pah-rah-sawl
– un bateau. aN bah-to

I'd like to take a *diving / windsurfing* course.

Je veux bien reçevoir des instructions *de plongée / de windsurf*. zhuh vuh bee-aN ruh-suh-vwahr day-zaN-strewk-see-ohn *duh plohN-zheh / duh wind-surf*

How much is it per *hour / day*?

Quel est le tarif pour *une heure / une journée*? kel eh luh tah-reef poor *ewn uhr / ewn zhoor-nay*

Would you mind watching my things for a moment, please?

Vous pourriez surveiller mes affaires un instant, s'il vous plaît? voo poor-ee-eh sewr-veh-yeh may-zah-fehr aN-naN-stahN see voo play

Is there an *indoor / outdoor* pool here?

Est-ce qu'il y a une piscine *couverte / découverte* ici? es keel yah ewn pee-seen *koo-vehrt / day-koo-vehrt* ee-see

What change do I need for the *lockers / hair dryers*?

Pour le *vestiaire / sèche-cheveux*, qu'est-ce qu'il me faut comme pièces? poor luh *ves-tyehr / sehsh-shuh-vuh* kes-keel muh fo kum pee-yes

I'd like to *rent / buy* …

Je voudrais *louer / acheter* … zhuh voo-dreh *loo-eh / ahsh-teh*

– a swimming cap.

– un bonnet de bain. aN bun-eh duh baN

– swimming goggles.

– des lunettes de piscine. day lewn-et duh pee-seen

– towel.

– une serviette de bain. ewn sehr-vyet duh baN

Where's the *pool attendant / first-aid station*?

Où est le *maître-nageur / poste de secours*? oo eh luh *meh-truh-nah-zhuhr / pawst duh suh-koor*

Beach and Pool: Additional Words

arm floats	les brassards *m/pl* de natation
	lay brah-sahr duh nah-tah-see-ohN
beach	la plage lah plahzh
beach ball	le ballon de plage
	luh bah-lohN duh plahzh

boat rentals	la location de bateaux lah lo-kah-see-ohN duh bah-to
changing room	la cabine lah kah-been
to dive	plonger plohN-zheh
diving equipment	l'équipement *m* de plongée lay-keep-mahN duh plohN-zheh
diving mask	les lunettes *f/pl* de plongée lay lewn-et duh plohN-zheh
to fish	pêcher peh-sheh
flippers	les palmes *f/pl* lay pahlm
high tide	la marée haute lah mah-ray oht
jet ski	le scooter des mers luh skoo-tuhr day mehr
lake	le lac luh lahk
life preserver	la bouée de sauvetage lah boo-eh duh sohv-tahzh
low tide	la marée basse lah mah-ray bahss
motorboat	le bateau à moteur luh bah-to ah mo-tuhr
non-swimmers	le non-nageur luh nohN-nah-zhuhr
nude beach	la plage naturiste lah plahzh nah-tew-reest
ocean	la mer lah mehr
pedal boat	le pédalo luh pay-dah-lo
row boat	le bateau à rames luh bah-to ah rahm
(rubber) raft	le bateau pneumatique luh bah-to pnuh-mah-teek
to sail	faire de la voile fehr duh lah vwahl
sail boat	le voilier luh vwahl-yeh
sand	le sable luh sah-bluh
sea urchin	l'oursin *m* loor-saN
shade	l'ombre *f* lohN-bruh
shells	les coquillages *m/pl* lay co-kee-yahzh

shower	la douche lah doosh
snorkel	le tube de plongée luh tewb duh plohN-zheh
storm warning	l'avis *m* de tempête lah-vee duh tahN-pet
sun	le soleil luh so-lay
sunglasses	les lunettes *f/pl* de soleil lay lewn-et duh so-lay
sunscreen	la crème solaire lah krem so-lehr
surfboard	la planche à voile lah plahNsh ah vwahl
to swim, bathe	se baigner suh ben-yeh
to swim	nager nah-zheh
swimming area	la plage gardée lah plahzh gahr-day
swimming pool	la piscine lah pee-seen
water	l'eau *f* lo
water ski	le ski nautique luh ski no-teek
wave	la vague lah vahg
wave pool	la piscine à vagues lah pee-seen ah vahg

Games

Do you mind if I join in?	Je peux jouer avec vous? zhuh puh zhoo-eh ah-vek voo
We'd like to rent a squash court for (half) an hour.	Nous voudrions retenir un court de squash pour une (demi-)heure. noo voo-dree-ohN ruh-ten-eer aN koor duh squash poor ewn (duh-mee) uhr
We'd like to rent a tennis court for an hour.	Nous voudrions retenir un court de tennis pour une heure. noo voo-dree-ohN ruh-ten-eer aN koor duh ten-neess poor ewn uhr
Where can you *go bowling* / *play pool* here?	Oú es-ce qu'on peut jouer au *bowling* / *billard*? oo es kohN puh zhoo-eh o *bowling* / *bee-yahr*
I'd like to rent …	Je voudrais louer … zhuh voo-dreh loo-eh

Games: Additional Words

badminton	le badminton luh bahd-mee-tohN
badminton racket	la raquette de badminton lah rah-ket duh bahd-meen-tohN
ball	un ballon aN bah-lohN
basketball	le basket luh bahs-ket
beach volleyball	le beach-volley luh beach-vawl-eh
bowling alley	le bowling luh bow-ling
double	le double luh doo-bluh
game	le jeu luh zhuh
goal	les buts *m/pl* lay bew
goalkeeper	le gardien de but luh gahr-dee-aN duh bew
golf	le golf luh gawlf

142

golf ball	la balle de golf lah bahl duh gawlf
golf club	le club de golf luh cluhb duh gawlf
golf course	le terrain de golf
	luh tehr-raN duh gawlf
handball	le handball luh ahNd-bahl
to lose	perdre pehr-druh
miniature golf course	le mini-golf luh mee-nee-gawlf
to play	jouer zhoo-eh
referee	l'arbitre m lahr-bee-truh
shuttlecock	le volant luh vo-lahN
single	le simple luh saN-pluh
soccer ball	le football luh fooht-bahl
soccer field	le terrain de football
	luh tehr-raN duh fooht-bahl
soccer game	le match de football
	luh mahtch duh fooht-bahl
squash	le squash luh squash
squash ball	la balle de squash
	lah bahl duh squash
squash racket	la raquette de squash
	lah rah-ket duh squash
table tennis	le ping-pong luh ping-pohN
team	l'équipe f lay-keep
tennis	le tennis luh ten-eess
tennis ball	la balle de tennis
	lah bahl duh ten-eess
tennis racket	la raquette de tennis
	lah rah-ket duh ten-eess
(a) tie	match nul mahtch newl
umpire	l'arbitre m lah-bee-truh
victory	la victoire lah veek-twahr
volleyball	le volley luh vol-lay
to win	gagner gahn-yeh

Indoor Activities

Do you have any *playing cards / board games*?

Vous avez des *cartes à jouer / jeux de société*? voo-zah-veh day *kahrt ah zhoo-eh / zhuh duh so-see-eh-teh*

Do you play chess?

Vous jouez aux échecs? voo zhoo-eh o-zeh-shek

Is there a *sauna / gym* here?

Est-ce qu'il y a un *sauna / club de sport* ici? es-keel yah aN *so-nah / klahb duh spawr* ee-see

Do you offer *aerobics / exercise* classes as well?

Est-ce que vous proposez aussi des cours d'*aérobic / de gymnastique*? es kuh voo pro-poh-zeh o-see day koor *dah-ehr-o-beek / duh zheem-nahs-teek*

Sports

Hiking

Can you recommend an easy tour?

Vous pourriez me recommander une randonnée facile? voo poor-ee-eh muh ruh-kohN-mahN-day ewn rahN-dun-eh fah-seel

About how long will it take?

Combien de temps dure-t-elle environ? kohN-bee-aN duh tahN dewr-tel ahN-vee-rohN

Is the trail *well marked / safe for walking*?

Le chemin est bien *balisé / protégé*? luh shuh-maN eh bee-aN *bah-lee-zeh / pro-teh-zheh*

Can I go in these shoes?

Est-ce que je peux y aller avec ces chaussures? es kuh zhuh puh ee ah-lay ah-vek say sho-sewr

Are there guided walks?	Est-ce qu'il y a des randonnées guidées? es keel yah day rahN-dun-eh ghee-day
What time's the last train?	A quelle heure descend le dernier téléphérique? ah kel uhr day-sahN luh dehrn-yeh teh-lay-feh-reek
Is this the right road for …?	Est-ce-que c'est bien la bonne route pour …? es kuh say bee-aN lah bun root poor
How far is it to …?	C'est encore loin jusqu'à …? say ahN-kaw lawn zhews-kah

Hiking: Additional Words

aerial tramway	le téléphérique luh teh-lay-feh-reek
chair lift	le télésiège luh teh-lay-see-yehzh
to climb	escalader es-kah-lah-day
climbing boots	les chaussures *f/pl* de montagne lay sho-sewr duh mohN-tahn-yuh
crampon	les crampons *m/pl* lay krahN-pohN
food	les vivres lay vee-vruh
to have a good head for heights	ne pas avoir le vertige nuh pah-zah-vwahr luh vehr-teezh
to hike	faire des randonnées fehr day rahN-dun-eh
hiking trail	le sentier de randonnée luh sahN-tyeh duh rahN-dun-eh
hut	le chalet luh shal-lay
to jog	faire du jogging fehr dew zhawg-ing
jogging	le jogging luh zhawg-ing
mountain	la montagne lah mohN-tahn-yuh
mountain climbing	l'alpinisme *m* lahl-peen-eez-muh

145

mountain guide	le guide de montagne
	luh gheed duh mohN-tahn-yuh
mountain rescue	les secours *m/pl* (en montagne)
service	lay suh-koor (ahN mohN tahn-yuh)
path	le chemin luh shuh-maN
ravine	les gorges *f/pl* lay gawrzh
rope	la corde la kawrd
shelter	le refuge luh ruh-fewzh
summit	le sommet luh sum-may
walkers' map	la carte de randonnée
	lah kahrt duh rahN-dun-eh
walking shoes	les chaussures *f/pl* de randonnée
	lay sho-sewr duh rahN-dun-ay
walking sticks	les cannes *f/pl* lay kahn

Bicycling

I'd like to rent a
bicycle / mountain bike.

Je voudrais louer *un vélo / une
mountain bike.* zhuh voo-dreh loo-eh
aN veh-lo / ewn moun-tain bike

I'd like a bike with …
gears.

Je voudrais un vélo avec … vitesses.
zhuh voo-dreh aN veh-lo ah-vek …
vee-tess

Do you have a bicycle
with a backpedal
brake?

Avez-vous aussi un vélo avec
rétropédalage? ah-veh-voo o-see aN
veh-lo ah-vek ray-tro-pay-dah-lahzh

I'd like to rent it for …

Je voudrais le louer pour …
zhuh voo-dreh luh loo-eh poor

– one day.
– two days.
– a week.

– une journée. ewn zhoor-nay
– deux jours. duh zhoor
– une semaine. ewn suh-men

Could you adjust the saddle for me?

Pourriez-vous me régler la hauteur de la selle? poor-ee-eh-voo muh ray-glay lah o-tuhr duh lah sel

Please give me a helmet as well.

Donnez-moi aussi un casque (de vélo), s'il vous plaît. dun-eh–mwah o-see aN kahsk (duh veh-lo) see voo play

Do you have a map?

Vous avez une carte?
voo-zah-veh ewn kahrt

Bicycling: Additional Words

back light	le feu arrière luh fuh ah-ree-yehr
bicycle repair kit	le set de réparation pour vélo luh set duh ray-pah-rah-see-ohN poor veh-lo
bike basket	le panier porte-bagages luh pahn-yeh pawt-bah-gahzh
child seat	le siège pour enfant luh see-yehzh poor ahN-fahN
child's bicycle	le vélo pour enfant luh veh-lo poor ahN-fahN
cycling path	la piste cyclable lah peest see-klah-bluh
front light	le feu avant luh fuh ah-vahN
hand brake	le frein à main luh fraN ah maN
inner tube	la chambre à air lah shahN-bruh ah ehr
light	le feu luh fuh
pump	la pompe à air lah pohNp ah ehr
saddle	la selle lah sel
saddlebags	les sacoches f/pl lay sah-kawsh
tire	le pneu luh puh-nuh

tire pressure	la pression des pneus
	lah press-see-ohN day puh-nuh
valve	la valve lah vahlv

Adventure Sports

ballooning	le ballon luh bah-lohN
bungee jumping	le saut à l'élastique
	luh so-tah lay-lahs-teek
canoe	le canoë luh kah-noh-eh
free climbing	la varappe lah vah-rahp
glider	le planeur luh plah-nuhr
gliding	le vol à voile luh vawl ah vwahl
kayak	le kayak luh kah-yahk
paragliding	le parapente luh pah-rah-pahNt
regatta	la régate lah ray-gaht
river rafting	le rafting luh rahf-ting
row boat	le bateau à rames
	luh bah-to ah rahm
skydiving	le saut en parachute
	luh soht ahN pah-rah-shewt
thermal current	le courant ascensionnel
	luh koo-rahN-tah-sahN-see-o-nel
to ride (horseback)	faire du cheval fehr dew shuh-vahl
to sail	faire de la voile fehr duh lah vwahl

Beauty

At the Salon

| I'd like an appointment for … . | J'aimerais bien avoir rendez-vous pour … . zhem-eh-reh bee-aN ah-vwahr rahN-day-voo poor |

Qu'est-ce qu'on vous fait?	What are you having done?
I'd like …	Je voudrais … zhuh voo-dreh
– a haircut.	– me faire couper les cheveux. muh fehr koo-pay lay shuh-vuh
– a perm.	– une permanente. ewn pehr-mah-nahNt
– some highlights.	– le balayage luh bah-lah-yahzh
– my hair colored.	– une teinture. ewn taN-tewr
Cut, shampoo and blow-dry, please.	Une coupe, un shampooing et un brushing, s'il vous plaît. ewn koop aN shaN-pwahN eh aN bruh-shing see voo play
Just a trim, please.	Une coupe seulement, s'il vous plaît. ewn koop suhl-mahN see voo play
Que désirez-vous comme coupe?	How would you like it?
Not too short, please.	Pas trop court, s'il vous plaît. pah tro koor see voo play
A bit shorter, please.	Un peu plus court, s'il vous plaît. aN puh plew koor see voo play
A short crop, please.	Très court, s'il vous plaît. treh koor see voo play
in the back	derrière dehr-yehr
in the front	devant duh-vahN
at the sides	de côté duh ko-teh
on top	en haut ahN oh

149

| The part on the *left / right*, please. | La raie à *gauche / droite*, s'il vous plaît. lah ray ah *gosh / drwaht* see voo play |
| Thanks, that's fine. | Merci beaucoup, c'est très bien. mehr-see bo-koo say treh bee-aN |

At the Salon: Additional Words

bangs	la frange lah frahNzh
beard	la barbe lah bahrb
black	noir nwahr
to blow-dry	faire un brushing fehr aN bruh-shing
blond	blond blohN
brown	brun braN
curls	les boucles *f/pl* (de cheveux) lay boo-kluh (duh shuh-vuh)
dandruff	les pellicules *f/pl* lay pel-ee-kewl
to dye	faire une teinture fehr ewn taN-tewr
gel	le gel luh zhel
gray	gris gree
hair	les cheveux *m/pl* lay shuh-vuh
hairspray	la laque à cheveux lah lahk ah shuh-vuh
hairstyle	la coiffure lah kwah-fewr
layers	la coupe en dégradé lah koop ahN day-grah-day
mousse	la mousse coiffante lah moos kwah-fahNt
moustache	la moustache lah moos-tahsh
shampoo	le shampooing luh shahN-pwahN
to shave	raser rah-zeh
to wash	faire un shampooing fehr aN shahN-pwahN

Beauty Treatments

I'd like a facial please.

Je voudrais un soin du visage.
zhuh voo-dreh aN swaN dew vee-sahzh

I've got …

J'ai … zhay

– normal skin.

– une peau normale.
ewn po naw-mahl

– oily skin.

– une peau grasse. ewn po grahss

– dry skin.

– une peau sèche. ewn po sehsh

– combination skin.

– une peau mixte. ewn po meext

I have sensitive skin.

J'ai une peau sensible.
zheh ewn po sahN-see-bluh

Please use only
fragrance-free /
hypoallergenic
products.

N'utilisez que des produits *sans
parfum* / *dermatologiquement
testés*, s'il vous plaît. new-tee-lee-zeh
kuh day pro-dwee *sahN pahr-faN* / *dehr-
mah-toh-lo-zheek-mahN tes-teh* see voo
play

Could you tweeze my
eyebrows?

Est-ce que vous pouvez m'épiler les
sourcils? es kuh voo poo-veh may-pee-
leh lay soor-see

I'd like to have my
eyelashes / *eyebrows*
dyed.

Je voudrais me faire teindre les
cils / *sourcils*. zhuh voo-dreh muh fehr
taN-druh lay *see* / *soor-see*

I'd like a half leg wax.

Je voudrais une épilation de la
demi jambe, s'il vous plaît.
zhuh voo-dreh ewn eh-pee-lah-see-ohN
duh lah duh-mee zhahNb see voo play

A *manicure* / *pedicure*,
please.

Une *manucure* / *pédicure*, s'il vous
plaît. ewn *mahn-ew-cewr* / *pay-dee-
kewr* see voo play

Beauty Treatments: Additional Words

cleansing	le nettoyage luh net-wah-yahzh
face	le visage luh vee-sahzh
mask	le masque luh mahsk
moisturizing mask	le masque hydratant luh mahsk ee-drah-tahN
neck	le cou luh koo
neck and chest	le décolleté luh day-kol-teh
peeling	le peeling luh pee-ling

Well-Being

acupuncture	l'acuponcture f lah-kew-pohNk-tewr
massage	le massage luh mah-sahzh
mud mask	la boue lah boo
purification	l'épuration f lay-pew-rah-see-ohN
reflexology massage	le massage des zones de réflexe du pied luh mah-sahzh day zohn duh ray-flex dew pyeh
sauna	le sauna luh so-nah
tanning salon	le solarium luh so-lah-ree-um
yoga	le yoga luh yo-gah

Things to Do

Where's the tourist information office?
Où se trouve l'office du tourisme?

How much are the tickets?
Combien coûtent les billets?

Sightseeing

info The French Government Tourist Offices are often located in the town center (centre-ville). Their website Maison de la France (www.franceguide.com) also provides valuable information.

Tourist Information

Where's the tourist information office?	Où se trouve l'office du tourisme? oo suh troov law-feess dew toor-eez-muh
I'd like …	Je voudrais … zhuh voo-dreh
– a map of the area.	– un plan des environs. aN plahN day-zahN-vee-rohN
– a map of the town.	– un plan de la ville. aN plahN duh lah veel
– a subway map.	– un plan du métro. aN plahN dew may-troh
– an events guide.	– un calendrier des manifestations. aN kah-lahN-dree-eh day mahn-ee-fes-tah-see-ohN
Do you have a brochure in English?	Avez-vous une brochure en anglais? ah-veh-voo ewn bro-shewr ahN ahN-gleh
I'd like to visit …	J'aimerais bien visiter … zhem-eh-reh bee-aN vee-zee-teh
Are there *sightseeing tours of the town* / *guided walks around the town*?	Est-ce qu'il y a des *tours guidés de la ville* / *visites guidées de la ville*? es keel yah day *toor ghee-day duh lah veel* / *vee-zeet ghee-day duh lah veel*

How much is the *sightseeing tour / guided walk*?

Combien coûte *le tour guidé / la visite guidée*? kohN-bee-aN koot *luh tour ghee-day / lah vee-zeet ghee-day*

How long does the *sightseeing tour / guided walk* take?

Combien de temps dure *le tour guidé / la visite guidée*? kohN-bee-aN duh tahN dewr *luh toor ghee-day / lah vee-zeet ghee-day*

A ticket / Two tickets for the sightseeing tour, please.

***Un billet / Deux billets*, s'il vous plaît, pour le tour guidé de la ville.** *aN bee-yeh / duh bee-yeh* see voo play poor luh toor ghee-day duh lah veel

What are the places of interest around here?

Qu'est-ce qu'il y a à voir ici? kes keel yah ah vwahr ee-see

One ticket / Two tickets for tomorrow's excursion to ..., please.

***Une place / Deux places* pour l'excursion de demain à ..., s'il vous plaît.** *ewn plahss / duh plahss* poor lek-scewr-zee-ohN ah ... see voo play

When / Where do we meet?

***Quand / Où* est-ce que nous nous rencontrons?** *kahN / oo* es kuh noo noo rahN-kohN-trohN

Do we also visit ...?

Est-ce que nous allons aussi visiter ...? es kuh noo-zahl-ohN o-see vee-zee-teh

When do we get back?

A quelle heure revenons-nous? ah kel uhr ruh-vuh-nohN noo

Accommodations, page 23;
Asking for Directions, page 38;
Public Transportation, page 59

Excursions and Sights

When is ... open?

Quelles sont les heures d'ouverture de ...? kel sohN lay-zuhr doo-vehr-tewr duh

What's the admission charge?

Combien coûte l'entrée?
kohN-bee-aN koot lahN-tray

How much is the tour?

Combien coûte cette excursion?
kohN-bee-aN koot set ek-scewr-zee-ohN

Are there guided tours in English?

Y a-t-il des tours guidés an anglais?
ee-ah-teel day toor ghee-day ahN ahN-gleh

Are there discounts for …	Est-ce qu'il y a une réduction pour … es keel yah ewn ray-dewk-see-ohN poor
– families?	– les familles? lay fah-mee
– children?	– les enfants? lay-zahN-fahN
– senior citizens?	– les personnes du troisième âge? lay pehr-sun dew trwah-zee-em ahzh
– students?	– les étudiants? lay-zeh-tew-dyahN
When does the guided tour start?	A quelle heure commence la visite? ah kel uhr kohN-mahNz lah vee-zeet
Two adults and two children, please.	Deux adultes, deux enfants, s'il vous plaît. duh-zah-dewlt duh-zahN-fahN see voo play
Are we allowed to take photographs?	Est-ce qu'on a le droit de prendre des photos? es kohN ah luh drwah duh prahN-druh day fo-toh

Excursions and Sights: Additional Words

abbey	l'abbaye f lah-bay
altar	l'autel m lo-tel
aqueduct	l'aqueduc m lah-kuh-dewk
area	la région lah ray-zhee-ohN
art	l'art m lahr
art collection	la collection de peintures lah col-ek-see-ohN duh paN-tewr
artist	l'artiste m, f lahr-teest
baroque	le baroque luh bah-rawk
bell	la cloche lah klawsh
bell tower	le clocher luh klaw-shay
botanical gardens	le jardin botanique luh zhahr-daN bo-tah-neek

157

brewery	la brasserie lah brahs-suh-ree
bridge	le pont luh pohN
brochure	le catalogue luh kah-tah-lawg
building	l'édifice *m* lay-dee-feess
bust	le buste luh bewst
capital	la capitale lah kah-pee-tahl
carving	la sculpture sur bois
	lah skewlp-tewr sewr bwah
castle	le château luh shah-toh
cathedral	la cathédrale lah kah-teh-drahl
Catholic	catholique kah-toh-leek
cave	la grotte lah grawt
ceiling	le plafond luh plah-fohN
Celtic	celtique sel-teek
cemetery	le cimetière luh seem-tyehr
ceramic	la céramique lah seh-rah-meek
chapel	la chapelle lah shah-pel
chimes	le carillon luh kah-ree-yohN
choir	le chœur luh kuhr
church	l'église *f* lay-gleez
church service	l'office *m* religieux
	law-feess ray-lee-zhyuh
church tower	le clocher luh klaw-shay
classical; ancient	antique ahN-teek
cloisters	le cloître luh klwah-truh
closed	fermé fehr-may
collection	la collection lah ko-lek-see-ohN
convent	le couvent luh koo-vahN
copy	la copie lah kaw-pee
court	la cour la coor
cross	la croix lah krwah
dome	la coupole lah koo-pohl
drawing	le dessin luh day-saN
excavations	les fouilles *f/pl* lay foo-yuh
exhibition	l'exposition *f* lex-po-zee-see-ohN

158

facade	la façade lah fah-sahd
to film	filmer feelm-eh
flea market	le marché aux puces luh mahr-shay o pewss
folk museum	le musée des arts populaires luh mew-zee day-zahr paw-pewl-lehr
forest	la forêt lah for-eh
fortress	le fort luh fawr
fountain	la fontaine lah fohN-ten
fresco	la fresque lah fresk
gallery	la galerie la gah-luh-ree
garden	le jardin luh zhahr-daN
gate	la porte lah pawrt
grave	le gothique luh go-teek
hall	la salle lah sahl
harbor	le port luh pawr
hill	la colline lah kaw-leen
house	la maison lah may-sohN
indoor market	les halles *f/pl* lay ahl
inscription	l'inscription *f* laN-screep-see-ohN
island	l'île *f* leel
Jewish	juif zhweef
king	le roi luh rwah
lake	le lac luh lahk
landscape	le paysage luh pay-ee-sahzh
library	la bibliothèque lah bee-blee-o-tek
marble	le marbre luh mahr-bruh
market	le marché luh mahr-shay
mausoleum	le mausolée luh mo-so-lay
memorial	le site commémoratif luh seet kohN-mem-or-ah-teef
mill	le moulin luh moo-laN
model	la maquette lah mah-ket
modern	moderne mo-dehrn
monastery	le monastère luh mohN-ah-stehr

159

monument	le monument luh mohN-ew-mahN
mosaic	la mosaïque lah mo-zah-eek
mountain	la montagne lah mohN-tahn-yuh
mountains	les montagnes *f/pl* lay mohN-tahn-yuh
mural	la peinture murale lah paN-tewr mew-rahl
museum	le musée luh mew-zeh
national park	le parc national luh pahrk nah-see-o-nahl
nature preserve	le site naturel protégé luh seet nah-tew-rel pro-teh-zheh
obelisk	l'obélisque *m* lo-bel-eesk
observatory	l'observatoire *m* lawb-sehr-vah-twahr
old part of town	la vieille ville lah vee-yeh veel
open	ouvert oo-vehr
opera house	l'opéra *m* lo-pehr-ah
organ	l'orgue *m* lawrg
original	l'original *m* lo-ree-zhee-nahl
painter	le peintre luh paN-truh
painting	la peinture lah paN-tewr
palace	le palais luh pah-leh
panorama	le panorama luh pah-naw-rah-mah
park	le parc luh pahrk
part of town	le quartier luh kahr-tyeh
pedestrian zone	la zone piétonne lah zohn pyeh-ton
peninsula	la péninsule lah peh-naN-sewl
picture	le tableau luh tah-blo
pillar	la colonne lah ko-lon
planetarium	le planétarium luh plahn-eh-tah-reeum
portal	le portail luh pawr-tigh
portrait	le portrait luh pawr-treh
pottery	la poterie lah paw-tuh-ree

queen	la reine lah ren
ravine	les gorges *f* lay gawrzh
relief	le relief luh ruh-lyef
religion	la religion lah reh-lee-zhee-yohN
remains	les vestiges *m/pl* lay ves-teezh
renaissance	la Renaissance lah ruh-nay-sahNs
reservoir	le lac artificiel luh lahk ahr-tee-fee-see-el
restored	restauré res-toh-ray
river	la rivière lah ree-vyehr
ruins	les ruines *f/pl* lay rew-een
sandstone	le grès luh greh
sculptor	le sculpteur luh skewlp-tuhr
sculpture	la sculpture lah skewlp-tewr
sights	les curiosités *f/pl* lay kew-ree-aws-see-teh
square	la place lah plahss
stadium	le stade luh stahd
statue	la statue lah stah-tew
style	le style luh steel
surroundings	les environs *m/pl* lay-zahN-vee-rohN
synagogue	la synagogue lah see-nah-gawg
to take photographs	prendre des photos pahN-druh day fo-toh
temple	le temple luh tahN-pluh
theater	le théâtre luh teh-ah-truh
to visit	visiter vee-zee-teh
tour boat	la vedette d'excursion lah veh-det dek-scewr-zee-ohN
tourist guide	le guide luh gheed
tourist office	le syndicat d'initiative luh saN-dee-kah dee-nee-see-ah-teev
tower	la tour lah toor
town	la ville lah veel
town center	le centre-ville luh sahN-truh-veel

161

town gate	la porte de la ville
	lah pawt duh lah veel
town hall	l'hôtel *m* de ville lo-tel duh veel
town wall	les remparts *m/pl* lay rahN-pahr
treasury	le trésor luh treh-sawr
university	l'université *f* lewn-ee-vehr-see-teh
valley	la vallée lah vah-lay
vault	la voûte lah voot
view	la vue lah vew
wall	le mur luh mewr
waterfall	la cascade lah kas-kahd
window	la fenêtre lah fen-eh-truh
works	l'œuvre *f* luh-vruh
zoo	le zoo luh zo

Cultural Events

What's on *this* / *next* week?	Qu'est-ce qu'il y a *cette semaine* / *la semaine prochaine* comme manifestations? kes keel yah *set suh-men* / *lah suh-men pro-shen* kohm mahn-ee-fes-tah-see-ohN
Do you have a program of events?	Est-ce que vous avez un calendrier des manifestations? es kuh voo-zah-veh aN kah-lahN-dree-yeh day mahn-ee-fes-tah-see-ohN
Where can I get tickets?	Où est-ce qu'on prend les billets? oo es kohN prahN lay bee-yeh
When does ... start?	A quelle heure commence ... ah kel uhr kohm-ahNs
– the performance	– la représentation? lah ruh-pray-sahN-tah-see-ohN
– the concert	– le concert? luh kohN-sehr
– the film	– le film? luh feelm
When do the doors open?	A quelle heure est-ce qu'on ouvre les portes? ah kel uhr es kohN oo-vruh lay pawt
Can I reserve tickets?	On peut réserver? ohN puh ray-sehr-veh
I reserved tickets under the name of ...	J'ai réservé des places au nom de ... zheh ray-sehr-veh day plahss oh nohN duh
Do you have any tickets for *today* / *tomorrow*?	Vous avez encore des billets pour *aujourd'hui* / *demain*? voo-zah-veh ahN-kaw day bee-yeh poor *o-zhoor-dwee* / *duh-maN*

163

One ticket / Two tickets for ..., please.	*Un billet / Deux billets* pour ..., s'il vous plaît. *aN bee-yeh / duh bee-yeh poor... see voo play*
– today	– aujourd'hui o-zhoor-dwee
– tonight	– ce soir suh swahr
– tomorrow	– demain duh-maN
– the ... o'clock performance	– la séance de ... heures lah say-ahNs duh ... uhr
– the ... o'clock movie	– le film de ... heures luh feelm duh ... uhr
How much are the tickets?	Combien coûtent les billets? kohN-bee-aN koot lay bee-yeh
Are there discounts for ...	Est-ce qu'il y a une réduction pour ... es keel yah ewn ray-dewk-see-ohN poor
– children?	– les enfants? lay-zahN-fahN
– senior citizens?	– les personnes du troisième âge? lay pehr-sun dew trwah-zee-em ahzh
– students?	– les étudiants? lay-zeh-tew-dyahN
I'd like to rent a pair of opera glasses.	Je voudrais louer des jumelles. zhuh voo-dreh loo-eh day zhew-mel
What time does the performance end?	À quelle heure se termine la représentation? a kel uhr suh tehr-meen lah ruh-pray-sahN-tah-see-ohN

info Local papers and weekly entertainment guides tell you what's on. In Paris, look for L'Officiel des Spectacles and Pariscope.

At the Box Office

à droite	right
à gauche	left
complet	sold out
la caisse	box office
la galerie	balcony
la location	advance booking
la loge	box
la place	seat
la place debout	standing room ticket
le balcon	circle
le deuxième balcon	rear mezzanine
le milieu	center
le parterre	orchestra (seating)
le premier balcon	front mezzanine
le rang	row

Cultural Events: Additional Words

act	l'acte *m* lahkt
actor	l'acteur *m* lahk-tuhr
actress	l'actrice *f* lahk-treess
ballet	le ballet luh bah-leh
box office	la caisse lah kess
cabaret	le cabaret luh kah-bah-reh
choir	le chœur luh kuhr
circus	le cirque luh seerk
coatroom	le vestiaire luh ves-tehr
composer	le compositeur / la compositrice luh kohN-poz-ee-tuhr / lah kohN-poz-ee-treess
conductor	le chef d'orchestre luh shef daw-kes-truh

dancer	le danseur / la danseuse
	luh dahN-suhr / lah dahN-suhz
dubbed	postsynchronisé
	pawst-saN-kro-nee-zeh
evening of traditional music and dance	la soirée folklorique
	lah swah-ray folk-law-reek
feature film	le film luh feelm
festival	le festival luh fes-tee-vahl
intermission	l'entracte m lahN-trahkt
movie theater	le cinéma luh see-nay-mah
music	la musique lah mew-zeek
music recital	le récital de chant
	luh ray-see-tahl duh shahN
musical	la comédie musicale
	lah ko-may-dee mew-zee-cahl
open-air theater	le théâtre de plein air
	luh teh-ah-truh duh plen air
opening night	la première lah pruhm-yehr
opera	l'opéra m lo-peh-rah
operetta	l'opérette f lo-peh-ret
orchestra	l'orchestre m law-kes-truh
original version	la version originale
	lah vehr-zee-ohN o-ree-zhee-nahl
play	la pièce de théâtre
	lah pee-yes duh teh-ah-truh
pop concert	le concert pop luh kohN-sehr pawp
program	le programme luh pro-grahm
rock concert	le concert rock luh kohN-sehr rawk
seat	la place lah plahss
singer	le chanteur / la chanteuse
	luh shahN-tuhr / lah shahN-tuhz
subtitle	les sous-titres m/pl
	lay soo-tee-truh
theater	le théâtre luh teh-ah-truh
variety show	les variétés f/pl lay vah-ree-eh-teh

Nightlife

What's there to do here in the evening?	**Où est-ce qu'on peut sortir le soir par ici?** oo es kohN puh saw-teer luh swahr pahr ee-see
Where can you go dancing around here?	**Où est-ce qu'on peut aller danser par ici?** oo es kohN puh ah-lay dahN-say pahr ee-see
Is it for *young* / *older* people?	**On y rencontre plutôt *des jeunes* / *des adultes*?** ohN-ee rahN-kohN-truh plew-toh *day zhuhn* / *day-zah-dewlt*
Is evening attire required?	**Il faut se mettre en tenue de soirée?** ee fo suh met-truh ahN ten-ew duh swah-ray
Is this seat taken?	**Est-ce que cette place est prise?** es kuh set plahss eh pree-zuh
Do you serve refreshments here?	**Est-ce qu'on peut manger quelque chose ici?** es kohN puh mahN-zheh kel-kuh shoze ee-see
Could I see the wine list?	**Est-ce que vous avez la carte des vins?** es kuh voo-zah-veh lah cahrt day vaN

Eating and Drinking, page 77

What would you like to drink?	**Qu'est-ce que vous voulez boire?** kes-kuh voo voo-lay bwahr
A glass of wine, please.	**Un verre de vin, s'il vous plaît.** aN vehr duh vaN see voo play

*Asking Someone Out, page 17;
Flirting and Romance, page 18*

Would you like to dance?	Je peux vous inviter pour cette danse? zhuh puh voo-zahN-vee-teh poor set dahNs
You dance very well.	Vous dansez très bien. voo-dahNs-eh treh bee-aN

Nightlife: Additional Words

band	le groupe luh group
bar	le bar luh bahr
casino	le casino luh kah-zee-no
cocktail	le cocktail luh kawk-tail
dance	la soirée dansante lah swah-ray dahN-sahNt
drink	la boisson lah bwah-sohN
loud	bruyant brew-yahN

Money,
Mail and
Police

I'd like to cash a traveler's check.
Je voudrais encaisser un chèque de voyage.

Is there any mail for me?
Vous avez du courrier pour moi?

Money Matters

info The currency in France and Belgium is the euro, divided into 100 cents (centimes); the currency in Switzerland is the Swiss franc. Not all banks provide exchange services. Hotels sometimes do but only to their guests. Cash can also be obtained from ATMs with credit and ATM cards. Instructions are sometimes in English.

Excuse me, where's there a bank around here?	Pardon, vous pourriez m'indiquer une banque dans le coin? pahr-dohN voo poo-ree-eh maN-dee-keh ewn bahNk dahN luh kwaN
Where can I exchange some money?	Où est-ce que je peux changer de l'argent? oo es kuh zhuh puh shahNzh-eh duh lahr-zhahN
I'd like to change *dollars / pounds*.	Je voudrais changer des *dollars / livres*. zhuh voo-dreh shahNzh-eh day *dol-lahr / leev-ruh*
I'd like to cash a traveler's check.	Je voudrais encaisser un chèque de voyage. zhuh voo-dreh ahN-kess-eh aN shek duh vwah-yahzh
Votre passeport, s'il vous plaît.	Your passport, please.
Une signature ici, s'il vous plaît.	Sign here, please.
En quelle coupure voulez-vous votre argent?	How would you like it?

— Money, Mail and Police —

In small bills, please.
Donnez-moi des petites coupures, s'il vous plaît. dun-eh-mwah day puh-teet koo-pewr see voo play

Please give me some change as well.
Donnez-moi aussi un peu de monnaie. dun-eh-mwah o-see aN puh duh muh-nay

► Numbers, see inside front cover

Money Matters: Additional Words

amount	le montant luh mohN-tahN
automatic teller machine (ATM)	le distributeur de billets luh dee-stree-bew-tuhr duh bee-yeh
card number	le numéro de la carte luh new-may-ro duh lah kahrt
cash transfer	le virement (bancaire) luh veer-mahN (bahN-kehr)
check	le chèque luh shehk
coin	la pièce lay pee-yes
counter	la caisse lah kess
counter	le guichet luh ghee-shay
credit card	la carte de crédit lah kahrt duh kray-dee
currency	la valeur lah vah-luhr
currency exchange	le bureau de change luh bew-ro duh shahNzh
exchange rate	le cours luh koor
money	l'argent m lahr-zhahN
PIN	le code secret luh code suh-kreh
savings bank	la caisse d'épargne lah kess day-pahr-nyuh
signature	la signature lah seen-yah-tewr
transfer	le virement luh veer-mahN

171

Post Office

Where's the nearest *post office / mailbox*?	**Où est la *poste / boîte aux lettres* la plus proche?** oo eh lah *pawst / bwaht ah let-truh* lah plew prawsh
How much is a *letter / postcard* to …	**Combien coûte une *lettre / carte* pour …** kohN-bee-aN koot ewn *let-truh / kahrt* poor
A …-cent stamp, please.	**Un timbre à … centimes, s'il vous plâit.** aN taN-bruh ah … sahN-team see voo play
I'd like to send this letter …, please.	**Cette lettre …, s'il vous plaît.** set let-truh … see voo play
– by airmail	**– par avion** pahr ahv-yohN
– special delivery	**– par exprès** pahr ex-press
– by regular mail	**– par voie maritime** pahr vwah mah-ree-teem
I'd like to send this package.	**Je voudrais poster ce colis.** zhuh voo-dreh paws-teh suh ko-lee
Is there any mail for me?	**Vous avez du courrier pour moi?** voo-zah-veh dew koor-ee-eh poor mwah

Post Office: Additional Words

address	**l'adresse** *f* lah-dress
addressee	**le destinataire** luh des-tee-nah-tehr
declaration of value	**la valeur déclarée** lah vah-luhr day-klah-ray
express letter	**la lettre exprès** lah let-truh ex-press

insured package	le colis à valeur déclarée
	luh ko-lee ah vah-luhr day-klah-ray
postcard	la carte postale lah kahrt paws-tahl
to send	envoyer ahN-vwah-yeh
small package	le paquet luh pah-keh
special stamp	le timbre spécial
	luh taN-bruh spay-see-ahl
stamp	le timbre(-poste) luh taN-bruh (pawst)
zip code	le code postal luh code paws-tahl

Police

Where's the nearest police station?	Où est le poste de police le plus proche? oo eh luh pawst duh po-leess luh plew prawsh
I'd like to report …	Je voudrais dénoncer … zhuh voo-dreh day-nohN-say
– a theft.	– un vol. aN vawl
– a mugging.	– une agression. ewn ah-gres-see-ohN
– a rape.	– un viol. aN vee-awl

▸ *Accidents, page 52*

My … has been stolen.	On m'a volé ♂ mon / ♀ ma … ohN mah-vaw-lay ♂ *mohN* / ♀ *mah*
I've lost …	J'ai perdu … zheh pehr-dew
My car's been broken into.	On a ouvert ma voiture par effraction. ohN-ah oo-vehr mah vwah-tewr pahr eh-frahk-see-ohN
I've been *cheated / beaten up*.	On m'a *dupé / agressé*. ohN mah *dew-pay / ah-gres-say*

173

I need a report for insurance purposes.	J'ai besoin d'une attestation pour mon assurance. zheh buh-zwaN dewn ah-tes-tah-see-oN poor mohN ah-sewr-rahNs
I'd like to speak to my *lawyer / consulate*.	Je voudrais parler *à mon avocat / avec mon consulat*. zhuh voo-dreh pahr-lay *ah mohN ah-vo-kah / ah-vek mohN kohN-sew-lah*
I'm innocent.	Je suis innocent. zhuh swee een-no-sahN
Vos papiers, s'il vous plaît.	Your identification, please.
Adressez-vous à votre consulat.	Please contact your consulate.

Police: Additional Words

accident	l'accident *m* lahk-see-dahN
car radio	l'autoradio *m* lo-toh-rah-dee-oh
counterfeit money	la fausse monnaie lah fohss mun-ay
handbag	le sac à main luh sahk ah maN
lost and found	le bureau des objets trouvés luh bew-ro day-zawb-zheh troo-veh
narcotics	la drogue lah drawg
pickpocket	le pickpocket luh peek-paw-ket
police	la police lah po-leess
policeman	le gendarme luh gahN-dahrm
stolen	volé vaw-lay
thief	le voleur luh vol-uhr
wallet	le portefeuille luh pawt-fuh-yuh
witness	le témoin luh teh-mwaN

Health

Where's the nearest pharmacy?
Où est la pharmacie la plus proche?

Please call an ambulance!
Appelez une ambulance s'il vous plaît!

Pharmacy

Where's the nearest pharmacy?	**Où est la pharmacie la plus proche?** oo eh lah fahr-mah-see lah plew prawsh
Do you have anything for …?	**Vous avez quelque chose contre …?** voo-zah-veh kel-kuh shoze kohN-truh

▶ *Illnesses and Complaints, page 186*

I need this medicine.	**J'ai besoin de ce médicament.** zheh buh-zwaN duh suh may-dee-kah-mahN
A small pack will do.	**Une petite boîte suffira.** ewn puh-teet bwaht sew-fee-rah
Ce médicament est uniquement délivré sur ordonnance.	You need a prescription for this medicine.
Nous ne l'avons pas en magasin.	I'm afraid we don't have that.
Nous devons le commander.	We'll have to order it.
When can I pick it up?	**Vous l'aurez quand?** voo loh-ray kahN
How should I take it?	**Comment est-ce que je dois le prendre?** kohN-mahN es kuh zhuh dwah luh prahN-druh

Medication Information

ingredients	composition
applications	indications thérapeutiques
contraindications	contre-indications

dosage instructions	posologie
infants	enfants
children (over/under ... years)	enfants (à partir de / jusqu'à ... ans)
pregnant women	femmes enceintes
adults	adultes
three times a day	trois fois par jour
one tablet / one caplet	un comprimé
ten drops	dix gouttes
one teaspoon	une cuillère à café
to be taken as directed	conformément aux prescriptions du médecin

directions	mode d'administration
dissolve on the tongue	laisser fondre dans la bouche
after meals	après les repas
before meals	avant les repas
on an empty stomach	à jeun
to be swallowed whole, unchewed	avaler sans croquer

application	indications (thérapeutiques)
external	externe
rectal	rectal
internal	interne
oral	oral

side effects	effets secondaires
may cause drowsiness	peut provoquer une somnolence
you are advised not to drive	peut provoquer des troubles de la vigilance sur la route

Medicine and Medications

adhesive bandage	**le pansement** luh pahNs-mahN
after sunburn lotion	**la pommade contre les coups de soleil** lah pum-ahd kohN-truh lay koo duh so-lay
anti-itch cream	**la pommade contre les démangeaisons** lah pum-ahd kohN-truh lay day-mahN-zheh-zohN
antibiotic	**l'antibiotique** *m* lahN-tee-bee-o-teek
antiseptic	**le désinfectant** luh day-saN-fek-tahN
antiseptic ointment	**la pommade cicatrisante** lah pum-ahd see-kah-tree-sahNt
birth control pill	**la pilule contraceptive** lah pee-lewl kohN-trah-sep-teev
circulatory stimulant	**le médicament pour la circulation du sang** luh may-dee-kah-mahN poor lah seer-kew-lah-see-ohN dew sahN
condoms	**les préservatifs** *m/pl* lay pray-sehr-vah-teev
cough medicine	**le sirop contre la toux** luh see-ro kohN-truh lah too
drops	**les gouttes** *f/pl* lay goot
ear drops	**les gouttes** *f/pl* **pour les oreilles** lay goot poor lay-zo-ray
elastic bandage	**la bande élastique** lah bahNd eh-lahs-teek
eye drops	**le collyre** luh kawl-leer
first-aid kit	**les pansements** *m/pl* lay pahNs-mahN
gauze bandage	**la bande de gaze** lah bahNd duh gahz

178

headache pills	les comprimés *m/pl* contre le mal de tête lay kohN-pree-may kohN-truh luh mahl duh tet
homeopathic	homéopathique o-may-o-pah-teek
indigestion tablets	les comprimés *m/pl* contre les maux d'estomac lay kohN-pree-may kohN-truh lay moh day-sto-mah
injection	la piqûre lah pee-kewr
insulin	l'insuline *f* laN-sew-leen
iodine	l'iode *m* lee-awd
laxative	le laxatif luh lahx-ah-teef
nose drops	les gouttes *f/pl* pour le nez lay goot poor luh nay
ointment for a sun allergy	la pommade (contre les allergies au soleil) lah pum-ahd (kohN-truh lay-zah-lehr-zhee o so-lay)
ointment for mosquito bites	la pommade contre les piqûres de moustiques lah pum-ahd kohN-truh lay pee-kewr duh moo-steek
painkiller	l'analgésique *m* lahn-ahl-zheh-seek
powder	la poudre lah poo-druh
prescription	l'ordonnance *f* law-dun-ahNs
sleeping pills	les somnifères *m/pl* lay sum-nee-fehr
something for …	le remède contre … luh ruh-may-dee kohN-truh
suppository	le suppositoire luh sew-paw-zee-twahr
tablets	les comprimés lay kohN-pree-may
thermometer	le thermomètre luh tehr-mo-meh-truh
throat drops	les cachets *m/pl* pour la gorge lay kah-shay poor luh gawrzh
tranquilizer	le calmant luh kahl-mahN

Illnesses and Complaints, page 186

Looking for a Doctor

Can you recommend a *doctor* / *dentist*?

Est-ce que vous pouvez me recommander un *médecin généraliste* / *dentiste*? es kuh voo poo-veh muh ruh-kohN-mahN-day aN *made-saN zhen-eh-rah-leest* / *dahN-teest*

Does *he* / *she* speak English?

Parle-t-*il* / *elle* anglais? pahrl-uh-*teel* / *tel* ahN-gleh

Where's *his* / *her* office?

Où est son cabinet? oo eh sohN kah-bee-nay

Can *he* / *she* come to see me?

Est-ce qu'il / *Est-ce qu'elle* pourrait venir me voir? es *keel* / *es-kel* poo-reh ven-eer muh vwahr

info You'll be expected to pay doctors and dentists on the spot. Make sure your health insurance covers you while abroad.

Please call *an ambulance* / *a doctor*!

Appelez *une ambulance* / *le S.A.M.U.*, s'il vous plaît. ah-play ewn ahN-bew-lahNs / luh ess ah em ew see voo play

My *husband* / *wife* is sick.

Mon mari / *Ma femme* est malade. *mohN-mah-ree* / *mah fahm* eh mah-lahd

Physicians

dentist   le dentiste   luh dahN-teest

dermatologist   le dermatologue luh dehr-mah-toh-lawg

doctor   le médecin   luh made-saN

ear, nose and throat doctor	l'oto-rhino-laryngologiste *m*
	lo-toh-ree-no-lah-raN-go-lo-zheest
eye specialist	l'oculiste *m* loh-kew-leest
female doctor	le médecin luh made-saN
female gynecologist	la gynécologue
	lah zheen-eh-kaw-lawg
gynecologist	le gynécologue
	luh zheen-eh-kaw-lawg
homeopathic doctor	le practicien de médecines
	parallèles luh prahk-tee-see-ahN
	duh made-seen pah-rah-lel
internist	le spécialiste des maladies internes
	luh spay-see-ah-leest day mah-lah-dee
	aN-tehrn
orthopedist	l'orthopédiste *m* lor-toh-pay-deest
pediatrician	le pédiatre luh pay-dee-ah-truh
physician	le médecin généraliste
	luh made-saN zhehn-nehr-ah-leest
urologist	l'urologue *m* lew-ro-lawg
veterinarian	le vétérinaire luh veh-teh-ree-nehr

➤ At the Dentist's, page 191

At the Doctor's Office

I've got a (bad) cold.	**J'ai un (gros) rhume.** zheh aN (gro) rewm
I've got …	**J'ai …** zheh
– a headache.	– **mal à la tête.** mahl ah lah tet
– a sore throat.	– **mal à la gorge.** mahl ah lah gawrzh
– a high temperature.	– **de la fièvre.** duh lah fee-ev-ruh
– the flu.	– **la grippe.** lah greep
– diarrhea.	– **la diarrhée.** lah dee ah-ray
I don't feel well.	**Je ne me sens pas bien.** zhuh muh sahN pah bee-aN
I'm dizzy.	**J'ai des vertiges.** zheh day vehr-teezh
My … hurts / hurt.	**J'ai mal à / aux …** zheh mahl ah / o

▶ Body Parts and Organs, page 184

It hurts here.	**J'ai mal ici.** zheh mahl ee-see

 Emergency calls:
SAMU (medical emergencies): 15
Police emergencies: 17
Fire emergencies: 18

I've vomited (several times).	**J'ai vomi (plusieurs fois).** zheh voh-mee (pluh-zee-uhr fwah)
I've got an upset stomach.	**J'ai l'estomac barbouillé.** zheh les-toh-mah bahr-boo-yeh
I fainted.	**J'ai perdu connaissance.** zheh pehr-dew kohN-nay-sahNs

I can't move my …

Je ne peux pas bouger ♂ *mon* / ♀ *ma*… zhuh nuh pew pah boo-zhay ♂ *moN* / ♀ *mah*

I've hurt myself.

Je me suis blessé.
zhuh muh swee bles-say

I fell.

Je suis tombé. zhuh swee tohN-bay

I've been *stung* / *bitten* by …

J'ai été *piqué* / *mordu* par …
zheh eh-teh *pee-keh* / *maw-dew* pahr

I'm allergic to penicillin.

Je suis allergique à la pénicilline.
zhuh swee-zah-lehr-zheek ah lah pen-ee-see-leen

I've got *high* / *low* blood pressure.

Je souffre d'*hypertension* / *hypotension*. zhuh soo-fruh *dee-pehr-tahN-see-ohN* / *dee-po-tahN-see-ohN*

I've got a pacemaker.

Je porte un pacemaker.
zhuh pawrt aN pace-may-kehr

I'm (… months) pregnant.

Je suis enceinte (de … mois).
zhuh swee-zaN-saNt (duh… mwah)

I'm diabetic.

Je suis diabétique.
zhuh swee dee-ah-bay-teek

Où avez-vous mal?

Where's the pain?

Ça vous fait mal ici?

Does it hurt here?

Ouvrez la bouche.

Open your mouth.

Montrez la langue.

Show me your tongue.

Enlevez le haut, s'il vous plaît.

Undress to the waist, please.

Nous devons vous faire une radio.

We'll have to X-ray you.

183

Inspirez profondément. Ne respirez plus.	Take a deep breath. Hold your breath.
Depuis quand avez-vous ces problèmes?	How long have you had this problem?
J'ordonne une prise de sang / d'urine.	I'll need a *blood / urine* sample.
Il faut vous opérer.	You'll have to have an operation.
Ce n'est rien de grave.	It's nothing serious.
Revenez *demain / dans ... jours.*	Come back *tomorrow / in ... days.*
Can you give me a doctor's note?	**Est-ce que vous pourriez me faire un certificat?** es kuh voo poor-ee-eh muh fehr aN sehr-tee-fee-kah
Do I have to come back?	**Est-ce que je dois revenir?** es kuh zhuh dwah ruh-ven-eer
Could you give me a receipt for my medical insurance?	**Pourriez-vous me donner une facture pour mon assurance, s'il vous plaît?** poor-ee-eh voo muh dun-eh ewn fahk-tewr poor mohN-nah-sewr-ahNs see voo play

Body Parts and Organs

abdomen	le ventre luh vahN-truh
ankle	la cheville lah shuh-vee
appendix	l'appendice *m* lah-pahN-dees
arm	le bras luh brah
back	le dos luh doh

184

bladder	la vessie lah ves-see
blood	le sang luh sahN
body	le corps luh kawr
bone	l'os *m* loss
bottom	le séant luh say-ahN
brain	le cerveau luh sehr-vo
bronchial tubes	les bronches *f/pl* lay brohNsh
calf	le mollet luh maw-leh
chest	la poitrine lah pwah-treen
collarbone	la clavicule lah klah-vee-kewl
disc	le disque intervertébral luh deesk aN-tehr-vehr-teh-brahl
ear	l'oreille *f* lo-ray
eye	l'œil *m* les yeux *pl* luh-yuh lay-zyuh
face	le visage luh vee-zahzh
finger	le doigt luh dwah
foot	le pied luh pee-eh
forehead	le front luh frohN
frontal sinus	le sinus frontal luh see-newss frohN-tahl
gall bladder	la bile lah beel
genitals	les organes *m/pl* génitaux lay-zor-gahn zheh-nee-toh
hand	la main lah maN
head	la tête lah tet
heart	le cœur luh kuhr
heel	le talon luh tah-lohN
hip	la hanche lah ahNsh
intestine	les intestins *m/pl* lay-zaN-tes-taN
joint	l'articulation *f* lahr-tee-kew-lah-see-ohN
kidney	le rein luh raN
knee	le genou luh zhen-oo
kneecap	la rotule lah ro-tewl
leg	la jambe lah zhahNb

185

liver	le foie luh fwah
lungs	les poumons *m/pl* lay poo-mohN
mouth	la bouche lah boosh
mucus membrane	la muqueuse lah mew-kuhz
muscle	le muscle luh mews-kluh
neck	le cou luh koo
neck	la nuque lah newk
nerve	le nerf luh nehr
nose	le nez luh nay
pelvis	le bassin luh bah-saN
rib	la côte lah kawt
shinbone	le tibia luh tee-bee-ah
shoulder	l'épaule *f* lay-pohl
sinus	le sinus luh see-newss
skin	la peau lah po
spine	la colonne vertébrale
	lah kol-un vehr-teh-brahl
stomach	l'estomac *m* less–toh-mah
tendon	le tendon luh than-dohN
throat	la gorge lah gawrzh
thyroid gland	la thyroïde lah teer-aw-eed
toe	l'orteil *m* lor-teh
tongue	la langue lah lahNg
tonsils	les amygdales *f/pl*
	lay-zah-mee-dahl
tooth	la dent lah dahN
vertebrae	la vertèbre lah vehr-teb-ruh

Illnesses and Complaints

abscess	l'abcès *m* lahb-seh
AIDS	le sida luh see-dah
allergy	l'allergie *f* lahl-ehr-zhee
angina	l'angine *f* lahN-zheen

appendicitis	l'appendicite *f* lah-pahN-dee-seet
asthma	l'asthme *m* lahsm
bite	la morsure lah mawr-sewr
bite, sting	la piqûre lah pee-kewr
blister	l'ampoule *f* lahN-pool
breathing problems	les difficultés à respirer
	lay dee-fee-kewl-teh ah res-pee-ray
broken	cassé kah-say
bronchitis	la bronchite lah brawn-sheet
bruise	la contusion lah kohN-tew-zee-ohN
burn	la brûlure lah brew-lewr
bypass	le by-pass luh by-pass
cancer	le cancer luh kahN-sehr
cardiac infarction	l'infarctus *m* laN-fahrk-tewss
chicken pox	la varicelle lah vah-ree-sel
chills	les frissons *m/pl* lay frees-sohN
circulatory problems	les troubles *m/pl* circulatoires
	lay troo-bluh seer-kew-lah-twahr
cold	le rhume luh rewm
colic	la colique lah kaw-leek
concussion	la commotion cérébrale
	lah koh-mo-see-ohN say-ray-brahl
conjunctivitis	la conjonctivite
	lah kohN-zhohNd-tee-veet
constipation	la constipation
	lah kohN-stee-pah-see-ohN
cough	la toux lah too
cramp	la crampe lah krahNp
cystitis	la cystite lah sees-teet
diabetes	le diabète luh dee-ah-bet
diarrhea	la diarrhée lah dee-ah-ray
disease	la maladie lah mah-lah dee
dislocated	luxé lewx-eh
dizziness	les vertiges *m/pl* lay vehr-teezh
fever	la fièvre lah fee-ev-ruh

187

flu	**la grippe** lah greep
food poisoning	**l'intoxication** *f* **alimentaire** laN-tawx-ee-kah-see-ohN ah-lee-mahN-tehr
fungal infection	**la mycose** lah mee-kawz
heart attack	**la crise cardiaque** lah kreez kahr-dee-ahk
heart problem	**l'anomalie** *f* **cardiaque** lahn-o-mah-lee kahr-dee-ahk
heartburn	**les brûlures** *f/pl* **(d'estomac)** lay brew-lewr (day-stoh-mah)
hemorrhoids	**les hémorroïdes** *f/pl* lay em-or-ro-eed
hernia	**la hernie** lah ehr-nee
herpes	**l'herpès** *m* lehr-pez
high blood pressure	**la haute tension** lah oht tahn-see-ohN
infection	**l'infection** *f* laN-fek-see-ohN
infectious	**contagieux** kohN-tah-zhee-uh
inflammation	**l'inflammation** *f* laN-flah-mah-see-ohN
injury	**la blessure** lah bles-sewr
kidney stones	**les calculs** *m/pl* **rénaux** lay kahl-kewl ray-noh
low blood pressure	**la basse tension** lah bahss tahn-see-ohN
lower back pain	**le lumbago** luh laN-bah-goh
malaria	**la malaria** lah mahl-ah-ree-ah
meningitis	**la méningite** lah may-nahN-geet
migraine	**la migraine** lah mee-gren
motion sickness	**le mal des voyages** luh mahl day vwah-ahzh
nausea	**le mal au cœur** luh mahl o kuhr
neuralgia	**la névralgie** lah nev-rahl-zhee

nose bleed	les saignements *m/pl* de nez lay sen-yuh-mahN duh nay
pacemaker	le pacemaker luh pace-make-ehr
periods	les menstruations *f/pl* lay mahN-strew-ah-see-ohN
pneumonia	la pneumonie lah pnuh-mun-ee
polio	la poliomyélite lah paw-lee-um-yeh-leet
pulled ligament	l'entorse *f* lahN-tors
pulled muscle	le claquage musculaire luh klah-kahzh mews-kew-lehr
pulled tendon	l'élongation *f* lay-lohN-gah-see-ohN
rash	l'éruption *f* cutanée lay-rewp-see-ohN kew-tahn-eh
rheumatism	le rhumatisme luh ree-mah-teez-muh
sciatica	la sciatique lah syah-teek
sexually transmitted disease (STD)	la maladie vénérienne lah mah-lah-dee veh-nay-ree-en
shock	le choc luh shawk
sprained	foulé foo-lay
sting	la piqûre lah pee-kewr
stomach ache	les maux *m/pl* d'estomac les mo day-stoh-mah
stomach ulcer	l'ulcère *m* à l'estomac lewl-sehr ah les-toh-mah
stroke	l'attaque *f* (d'apoplexie) lah-tahk (dah-po-plex-ee)
sunburn	le coup de soleil luh koo duh so-lay
sunstroke	l'insolation *f* laN-so-lah-see-ohN
swelling	l'enflure *f* lahn-flewr
tick bite	la piqûre de tique lah pee-kewr duh teek
tonsillitis	l'amygdalite *f* lah-mee-dah-leet
torn ligament	la déchirure des ligaments lah day-she-rewr day lee-gah-mahN

ulcer	l'ulcère lewl-sehr
vomiting	les vomissements *m/pl*
	lay vaw-meess-mahN
whooping cough	la coqueluche lah kaw-kel-ewsh
wound	la blessure lah bles-sewr

At the Hospital

| Is there anyone here who can speak English? | Est-ce qu'il y a quelqu'un qui parle anglais? es keel yah kel-kaN kee pahrl ahN-gleh |

▶ *At the Doctor's Office, page 182*

I'd rather have the operation in the US.	Je préfère me faire opérer aux États-Unis. zhuh pray-fehr muh fair o-pay-ray oh-zeh-tahs-ew-nee
I'm insured for repatriation expenses.	Mon assurance couvre les frais de rapatriement. mohN ah-sew-rahNs koov-ruh lay freh duh rah-pah-tree mahN
Please let my family know.	Prévenez ma famille, s'il vous plaît. pray-vuh-nay mah fah-mee see voo play
Nurse, could you help me, please?	♂ Infirmier / ♀ Infirmière, pouvez-vous m'aider, s'il vous plaît? aN-feerm-yehr / aN-feerm-yeh poo-veh-voo med-eh see voo play
Please give me *a painkiller / sleeping pill.*	Donnez-moi quelque chose *contre la douleur / pour dormir*, s'il vous plaît. dun-ay mwah kel-kuh-shoze *kohN-truh lah doo-luhr / poor dawr-meer* see voo play

At the Dentist's

This tooth hurts.

J'ai mal à cette dent.
zheh mahl ah set dahN

This tooth is broken.

La dent s'est cassée.
lah dahN seh kah-say

I've lost *a filling* / *a crown*.

J'ai perdu *un plombage* / *une couronne*. zheh pehr-dew aN *plohN-bahzh* / *ewn koor-un*

Could you do a temporary job on the tooth?

Est-ce que vous pourriez soigner la dent de façon provisoire? es kuh voo poor-ee-eh swan-yeh lah dahN duh fah-sohN pro-vee-swahr

Please don't pull the tooth.

S'il vous plaît, ne m'arrachez pas la dent. see voo play nuh mah-rah-sheh pah lah dahN

Give me an injection, please.

Faites-moi une injection, s'il vous plaît. fet-mwah ewn aN-zhek-see-ohN see voo play

Can you repair these dentures?

Pourriez-vous réparer cette prothèse? poor-ee-eh-voo ray-pah-ray set praw-tehz

Vous avez besoin …

You need …

– d'un bridge.
– d'un plombage.
– d'une couronne.

– a bridge.
– a filling.
– a crown.

Je dois extraire la dent.

I'll have to take the tooth out.

Rincez bien.

Rinse well.

Ne rien manger pendant deux heures.	Don't eat anything for two hours.

At the Dentist's: Additional Words

amalgam filling	l'amalgame *m* lah-mahl-gahm
braces	l'appareil *m* dentaire lah-pah-ray dahN-tehr
cavity	la carie lah kah-ree
composite filling	le composite luh kohN-po-zeet
dentures	le dentier luh dahN-tee-eh
gold filling	le plombage en or luh plohN-bahzh ahN-awr
gum infection	l'inflammation *f* de la gencive laN- flah-mah-see-ohN duh lah zhahN-seev
gums	la gencive lah zhahN-seev
impression	l'empreinte *f* lahN-praNt
inlay	l'inlay *m* leen-lay
jaw	la mâchoire lah mah-shwahr
nerve	le nerf luh nehr
periodontal disease	la parodontose lah pah-rah-dohN-toh-zuh
porcelain filling	le plombage en porcelaine luh plohN-bahzh ahN pawr-suh-len
root	la racine lah rah-seen
root canal	le traitement de la racine lah tret-mahN duh lah rah-seen
tartar	le tartre luh tahr-truh
temporary filling	le traitement provisoire luh tret-mahN pro-vee-zwahr
tooth	la dent lah dahN
wisdom tooth	la dent de sagesse lah dahN duh sah-zhess

Time and the Calendar

What time is it?
Quelle heure est-il?

It's one o'clock.
Il est une heure.

Time of the Day

What time is it?	Quelle heure est-il? kel uhr eh-teel
It's one o'clock.	Il est une heure. eel eh ewn uhr
It's two o'clock.	Il est deux heures. eel eh duh-zuhr
It's *noon / midnight*.	Il est *midi / minuit*. eel eh *mee-dee / meen-wee*
It's five after four.	Il est quatre heures cinq. eel eh kaht-ruhr saNk
It's a quarter after five.	Il est cinq heures et quart. eel eh saNk uhr eh kahr
It's 6:30.	Il est six heures et demie. eel eh see-zuhr eh duh-mee
It's twenty-five to four.	Il est quinze heures trente-cinq. eel eh kaNz-uhr trahNt-saNk

info In general, the 24-hour clock is used in France. This means, rather than saying, "It's 2:30", it is better to say "It's 14:30." (Il est quartorze heures et demi.)

It's a quarter to nine.	Il est neuf heures moins le quart. eel eh nuhv-uhr mwaN luh kahr
It's ten to eight.	Il est huit heures moins dix. eel eh weet uhr mwaN deess
At what time?	A quelle heure? ah kel uhr
At ten o'clock.	A dix heures. ah dee-zuhr
Until eleven (o'clock).	Jusqu'à onze heures. zhews-kah ohNz uhr

— Time and the Calendar —

From eight till nine.	**De huit heures à neuf heures.** duh weet-uhr ah nuhv-uhr
Between ten and twelve.	**Entre dix et douze.** ahN-truh deess eh dooz
In half an hour.	**Dans une demi-heure.** dahN-sewn duh-mee uhr
It's (too) late.	**Il est (trop) tard.** eel eh (tro) tahr
It's too early.	**Il est encore trop tôt.** eel eh ahN-kawr tro toe

► *Numbers, see inside front cover*

Time Expressions: Additional Words

15 minutes	**le quart d'heure** luh kahr-duhr
a month ago	**il y a un mois** eel yah aN mwah
afternoon	**l'après-midi** *m* lah-preh-mee-dee
at around noon	**à midi** ah mee-dee
at dawn	**à l'aube** ah lobe
at night	**la nuit** la nwee
day	**le jour** luh zhoor
early	**tôt** toe
evening	**le soir** luh swahr
for	**pour** poor
half an hour	**la demi-heure** lah duh-mee-uhr
hour	**l'heure** *f* luhr
in the afternoon	**l'après-midi** *m* lah-preh-mee-dee
in the evening	**le soir** luh swahr
in the morning	**le matin** luh mah-taN
in two weeks	**dans quinze jours** dahN kaNz zhoor
late	**tard** tahr
later	**plus tard** plew tahr
minute	**la minute** lah meen-ewt

195

month	**le mois** luh mwah
morning	**le matin** luh mah-taN
next year	**l'année** *f* **prochaine** lah-nay pro-shen
night	**la nuit** lah nwee
now	**maintenant** maN-tuh-nahN
recently	**il y a peu de temps** eel yah puh duh tahN
second	**la seconde** lah suh-kohNd
since	**depuis** duh-pwee
sometimes	**quelquefois** kel-kuh-fwah
soon	**bientôt** bee-aN-toe
the day after tomorrow	**après-demain** ah-preh-duh-maN
the day before yesterday	**avant-hier** ah-vahN-tyehr
this afternoon	**cet après-midi** set ah-preh-mee-dee
this morning	**ce matin** suh mah-taN
time	**le temps** luh tahN
today	**aujourd'hui** oh-zhoor-dwee
tomorrow	**demain** duh-maN
tonight	**ce soir** suh swahr
until	**jusqu'à** zhews-kah
week	**la semaine** lah suh-men
year	**l'année** *f* lah-nay
yesterday	**hier** yehr

Seasons

spring	**le printemps** luh praN-tahN
summer	**l'été** *m* lay-teh
autumn	**l'automne** *m* lo-tun
winter	**l'hiver** *m* lee-vehr

——Time and the Calendar——

Date

What's today's date?	**On est le combien aujourd'hui?** ohN es luh kohN-bee-aN oh-zhoor-dwee
Today's July 2nd.	**Aujourd'hui, on est le deux juillet.** oh-zhoor-dwee ohN-eh luh duh zhwee-eh
On the 4th of *this / next* month.	**Le quatre *de ce mois / du mois prochain*.** luh kah-truh *duh suh mwah / dew mwah pro-shaN*
Until March 10th.	**Jusqu'au dix mars.** zhews-koh dee mahrss
We're leaving on August 20th.	**Nous partons le vingt août.** noo pahr-tohN luh vaN oot

Days of the Week

Monday	**lundi** laN-dee
Tuesday	**mardi** mahr-dee
Wednesday	**mercredi** mehr-kruh-dee
Thursday	**jeudi** zhuh-dee
Friday	**vendredi** vahN-druh-dee
Saturday	**samedi** sahm-dee
Sunday	**dimanche** dee-mahNsh

Months

January	**janvier** zhahN-vee-eh
February	**février** feh-vree-eh
March	**mars** mahrss
April	**avril** ah-vreel
May	**mai** meh

June	**juin** zhwaN
July	**juillet** zhwee-eh
August	**août** oot
September	**septembre** sep-tahN-bruh
October	**octobre** aw-tawb-ruh
November	**novembre** no-vahN-bruh
December	**décembre** day-sahN-bruh

Holidays

All Saints' Day	**la Toussaint** lah too-saN
Ascension	**l'Ascension** *f* lah-sahN-see-ohN
Assumption	**l'Assomption** *f* lah-sohN-see-ohN
Christmas	**Noël** no-el
Christmas Day	**Noël (le vingt-cinq décembre)** no-el (luh vaN-saNk day-sahN-bruh)
Christmas Eve	**la veille de Noël** lah veh-yuh duh no-el
Corpus Christi	**la fête du Saint Sacrement** lah fet dew saN sah-kruh-mahN
Easter	**Pâques** pahk
Easter Monday	**le lundi de Pâques** luh laN-dee duh pahk
Good Friday	**le vendredi-saint** luh vahN-druh-dee saN
Labor Day (May 1)	**la Fête du Travail** lah fet dew trah-vah
Mardi Gras	**le mardi gras** luh mahr-dee grah
New Year's Day	**le jour de l'an** luh zhoor duh-lahN
New Year's Eve	**la Saint-Sylvestre** lah saN-seel-ves-truh
Pentecost	**la Pentecôte** lah pahNt-kawt

Weather
and
Environment

What's the weather going to be like today?
Quel temps va-t-il faire aujourd'hui?

Can you drink the water?
Est-ce que l'eau est potable?

Weather

What *nice / terrible* weather we're having today!

Quel *beau / mauvais* temps, aujourd'hui! kel *bo / mo-veh* tahN o-zhoor-dwee

What's the weather going to be like *today / tomorrow*?

Quel temps va-t-il faire *aujourd'hui / demain*? kel tahN vah-teel fehr *o-zhoor-dwee / duh-maN*

What's the weather forecast?

Que dit la météo? kuh dee lah may-teh-o

It is / It's going to be ...

Il *fait / va faire* ... eel *feh / vah fehr*

– nice.
– beau. bo

– bad.
– mauvais. mo-veh

– warm.
– chaud. sho

– hot.
– très chaud. treh sho

– cold.
– froid. frwah

– humid.
– lourd. loor

It's going to *rain / be stormy*.

Il va y avoir *de la pluie / un orage*. eel vah ee ah-vwahr *duh lah plwee / aN aw-rahzh*

The sun's shining.

Le soleil brille. luh so-lay bree-yuh

It's pretty windy.

Il y a pas mal de vent. eel yah pah mahl duh vahN

It's raining.

Il pleut. eel pluh

It's snowing.

Il neige. eel nehzh

What's the temperature?

Quelle est la température? kel eh lah tahN-pehr-ah-tewr

It's ... degrees (below zero).

Il fait ... degrés (au-dessous de zéro). eel feh ... duh-gray (o duh-soo duh zeh-ro)

───── Weather and Environment ─────

Weather: Additional Words

clear	clair klehr
climate	le climat luh klee-mah
cloud	le nuage luh new-ahzh
cloudy	nuageux new-ah-zhuh
cool	frais f, fraîche pl freh fresh
damp	humide ew-meed
dawn	l'aube f lobe
degrees	le degré luh duh-gray
drizzle	le crachin luh krah-shaN
dry	sec f, sèche pl sek sesh
dusk	le crépuscule luh kray-pews-kewl
fog	le brouillard luh broo-yahr
frost	le gel luh zhel
hail	la grêle lah grel
hazy	brumeux brew-muh
heat	la grosse chaleur lah gross shah-luhr
lightning	l'éclair m lay-klehr
moon	la lune lah lewn
rainy	pluvieux plew-vyuh
shower	l'averse f lah-vehrss
snow	la neige lah nehzh
star	l'étoile f lay-twahl
sun	le soleil luh so-lay
sunny	ensoleillé ahN-so-leh-yeh
thunder	le tonnerre luh tun-ehr
variable	capricieux kah-pree-see-uh
wet	mouillé moo-yeh
wind	le vent luh vahN

Environment

It's very loud here.

Ici, c'est très bruyant.
ee-see seh treh brew-yahN

Could you please shut off that noise?

Est-ce que vous pouvez arrêter ce bruit? es kuh voo poo-veh ah-ret-teh suh brew-ee

It smells bad here.

Ça ne sent pas très bon, ici.
sah nuh sahN pah treh bohN ee-see

Where's that smell coming from?

D'où vient cette odeur?
doo-vee-aN set o-duhr

Can you drink the water?

Est-ce que l'eau est potable?
es kuh lo eh po-tah-bluh

The *water / air* is polluted.

L'eau / L'air est pollué(e).
lo / lehr eh pawl-eweh

Is that dangerous?

Est-ce que c'est dangereux?
es kuh seh dahN-zheh-ruh